The Making of a Deaconess
The Next Chapter

Fran A. Jones

Highly Favored Publishing™
Bowie, Maryland

The Making of a Deaconess: The Next Chapter
Copyright © 2017 Fran A. Jones

No part of this publication may be reproduced, stored in a retrieval system, or transmitted, in any form, or by any means, electronic, mechanical, photocopying, recording, or otherwise, without the prior consent of the author.

For questions about permissions, bulk orders, or appearances, contact the author at deaconessfran@gmail.com.

To find out more about how you can fulfill your publishing dream, contact:

Highly Favored Publishing
Bowie, Maryland 20716
highlyfavoredpublishing@gmail.com
www.highlyfavoredpublishing.com
Highly Favored Publishing™ is a division of Highly Favored, L.L.C.

All Scripture references, unless otherwise noted, are from the King James Version of the Holy Bible.

Printed in the United States of America

ISBN 978-0-9989085-0-2

To the memory of our loving daughter,
Sandra Yvette Mitchell.
You will forever remain in our hearts.

ACKNOWLEDGMENTS

I give special appreciation and honor to all the wonderful people who brought this endeavor to fruition. First, and always, I give thanks and praises to my Lord and Savior Jesus Christ.

To my friend, my number one supporter, the love of my life, my loving husband Earnest. I want to express my sincere gratitude for all your help, now and in the past. You are truly my other wing. I thank God for the blessing of YOU! Thank you for your love.

To my sister and friend, Theresa McCoy, you are one in a million. Thank you for all the many hours and hard work you put into this publication to ensure excellence. Thank you!

To my son, Jerome, I have watched you grow over the years. However, my greatest joy is watching you grow in the Lord. It does not yet appear what you shall become. Keep your hand in the hand of the One who has the master plan. I am so proud of you for being a great son, husband, and father to my grandchildren.

To my loving daughter, Tina, God only knows how grateful and honored I am to have you as my daughter. I am so proud of you and the unique way you have allowed the Lord to use you to advance His kingdom. You are a special woman with a special gift that, in God's time, will be a blessing to me and the entire world. Until then, continue to strive, continue to dream, continue to march to the beat of your own drum, and continue to believe that you can *do all things through Christ that strengthens you.*

To my dynamic duo and the greatest grandchildren in the world, Anaiah and Kamau, please know that I love you both from the bottom of my heart. From the first time I laid eyes on you, I knew you both were gifts from God that would be a blessing to me and the world. My prayer is that as you pursue your specific passions in life, chase your wildest dreams, and seek to change the world for good you will remember The Source of all your blessings and live in a way that brings glory to God and points people to the cross of Christ.

I am so proud of the two of you, not for the many great things you have done, but simply for who you are. Go forth and change the world, but remember that only what you do for Christ will last! I love you eternally.

I extend my sincere gratitude and appreciation to my friend and pastor, Reverend Dr. John L. McCoy. The way that you encourage and inspire others to look deep inside themselves and pull out the gifts that God has placed in them is simply amazing. I believe, "The best is yet to come." Thank you, Pastor.

I would like to give special thanks to my wonderful church family at The Word of God Baptist Church. Thanks for embracing me and showing me love.

To my deaconess sisters at The Word of God Baptist Church: Janet Humphrey, Phyllis Berry, Pauline Daniel, Stacey Cobb-Smith, Bettie Hulley, Theresa McCoy, Minnie Outlaw, Lila Abraham, and Brenda Allen. Thank you for your love and support. Let us continue to deny ourselves, take up our cross, and follow Jesus' paradigm of ministry.

To the best publisher and editor that I know, Melvette Melvin Davis of Highly Favored Publishing. Thank you for the superb preparation of the manuscript for this project and turning it into a meticulous work of quality that superseded my imagination. When others said it could not be done—you took on the challenge. Thank you!

TABLE OF CONTENTS

Foreword	9
Preface	13
Introduction	17
Section I: The Making of a Deaconess: My Story	35
Application: The Making of a Deaconess: Your Story	62
Section II: The Making of a Deaconess: Biblical Ministry to Women	65
Application: Women Around the Well	71
Application: Women Caught in Adultery	75
Application: Abigail: The Woman Married to Nabal	79
Application: Ruth and Naomi: Women in Need of Friendship	84
Section III: Moving Forward in Ministry: How a Deaconess Can Make a Difference	89
Application: Moving Forward in Ministry	104
Application: Self-Esteem	112
Application: Power Begins with "P": Prayer	117
Application: Power Begins with "P": Patience	120
Application: Power Begins with "P": *Persistence*	125
Section IV: Prerequisites for Deaconesses in the Local Church	127
Application: Prerequisites for Deaconesses in the Local Church	143
Section V: The Service of Deaconesses	153
Application: The Service of Deaconesses	164
Afterword	167

Appendices 169
   Helpful Scriptural References for Counseling 171
   Consecration Examination: Sample 182
   Biography: Sample 189
   Deaconess Consecration Service: Sample 190
   Deaconesses Must be Servants 192

Notes 193

About the Author 195

Foreword

Fran Jones has served as president of the Deaconess Ministry of The Word of God Baptist Church in University Park, Maryland for over 25 years. Her lengthy tenure however, has not dimmed her vision, dulled her enthusiasm, or stifled her creativity. She was elevated to this key position at a time when women were relegated to merely doing the laundry of baptismal attire or the mundane task of preparing the elements for communion. It was a time when to serve as a deaconess, to a large degree, mostly meant "dumbing down" and being satisfied with sitting in white on Communion Sundays as a silent subset of the deacon board. Fran, however, bided her time with a burning in her bosom to make a difference. Her second book, *Moving Beyond the Communion Table*, was implicit of her vision to strengthen the church and empower women for the challenges lurking in the shadows of the 21st century. Symbolism was not enough for this woman of God. She wanted more and knew the church was capable of doing more. She knew in her generous, compassionate heart that the church needed to become relevant if it was to make any real difference in the diverse culture that awaited just beyond the horizon of Y2K. This publication is a result of her eagle-like vision of what the future was and now is.

Halfway through the first decade of this new century, as she dutifully served as president of the Deaconesses Ministry, Fran experienced the unthinkable—that which no mother should ever have to face. On a balmy, horrific Monday evening in July 2006, her oldest daughter was tragically murdered. However, out of the ashes of this heart-wrenching event arose a woman emboldened with the determination to minister to other women who have experienced similar devastation. In the wake of what has become one of many cold cases (unsolved homicides) of the nation's capital, her heart has been set aflame with a passion to empower young women with a sense of self-worth that will prevent them from becoming victimized by abusive men and a culture of violence that is heavily prevalent in our inner cities. What amazes me about Fran Jones, and what sets her apart from other mothers who have had to suffer the senseless murder of a child, is that she is not obsessed with discovering *who* murdered her daughter but rather *what* murdered her daughter. In reflection, she has discovered that the real culprit of the heinous deed that snuffed out the life of her beloved daughter was the serial murderer *Culture*. A culture that objectifies and minimizes the value of women. A culture that exploits women in the work place and, in some cases, discriminates against women in the worship place. A culture that still, in 2017, says to women to "stay in your place."

Sadly, through careful contemplation, research, and analysis, Fran discovered that this cold-blooded killer of her daughter has great influence in the modern church. Shamefully, this killer is often given a voice at 11 o'clock on Sunday mornings in the preaching that is designed to liberate the masses. Therefore, Fran Jones has developed a multi-faceted ministry that is designed to liberate both the victim and the victimizer from the heinous crimes that continue to plague our society and leave psychological scaring and spiritual carnage in its wake. Fran Jones has recognized that until the culture is transformed, its captives, male and female, Protestant and Catholic, will never truly be set free. As her pastor, I have personally witnessed Fran embrace both men and women, mothers and daughters, and fathers and sons who suffer from the culture of rape, abuse, degradation, and exploitation that frequently festers in this country and is too often given refuge in the house of God.

Therefore, as I have perused the pages of this publication, I hear the clarion call of a voice crying out in the wilderness of urban communities saying to the church of Jesus Christ that the Church of Jesus Christ is the essential component of the healing of a sick society. Fran's call is one of compassion, protection, equality, and sensitivity at an epoch in history that is increasingly brutal to vulnerable young women, patronizing to middle class women, and deadly to senior women in the twilight of their lives. With each turn of the pages of this publication I am overwhelmed with the work of Fran Jones, a woman who has dedicated her life to the uplift of the downtrodden and the strengthening of her suffering sisters. Fran Jones is more than a deaconess. She is a woman on a mission, and that mission is made plain in each chapter as she challenges the church to do more than merely have service on Sunday and passively pray on Wednesday evenings. No one reading her writing can doubt her motives as she goes about ministry. Fran's call is a noble endeavor, a just cause. Her call is to a cause whose time has come. I am amazed that at a time such as this God has given us Fran Jones, an untiring and determined woman. I encourage each reader to walk with her as she journeys through that quagmire of what the deaconess "board" used to be to where the deaconess "ministry" needs to be in a time unlike any other. I can only pray that this book will be well read because her mission is surely well said.

J. L. McCoy, Pastor
The Word of God Baptist Church

Preface

Since the first publication of *The Making of a Deaconess*, I have come to realize that deaconesses are not so much made, but birthed, and that birth is often via pain. In retrospect, I find that I have had many rebirths. These rebirths have made me more excited about and committed to the work of the deaconess than when first consecrated.

As I reflect upon the road that I have been traveling since the first publication, I am astonished to discover that each of my rebirths was also preceded by agonizing pain. The greatest pain, of course, that I have ever experienced in my greater than seven decades of living was the murder of my eldest daughter Sandra. There is simply no way that I can attempt to chronicle my life and not make reference to my personal 9/11. Her death destroyed so much of who I was. With her slaying, my first instinct was to hope that God would unleash great wrath upon the perpetrator of the dastardly deed that snuffed out her life just as she was in the final stages of recovery from drug addiction. However, ten years later, in the wake of my daughter's death, my feelings are much different than when first afflicted.

Even though sporadic, excruciating pain still throbs within my soul, it is my prayer that whoever took my daughter's life is apprehended and receives the treatment that is necessary to prevent another mother from experiencing the horrific crime that ended my daughter's life—and altered mine forever. I am determined to lobby for reform within the criminal justice system to develop programs of *real* rehabilitation. It takes no genius to surmise that our prison system is broken. Some even liken our institutions of incarceration are to "crime colleges," arguing they do more to teach and promote a criminal mindset than to rehabilitate. This is why, as a deaconess, as much as humanly possible, I vow to work with and within as many institutions in our society as possible that impact human behavior because as the saying goes, *when good men do nothing, evil prevails.* I also pray that the death of my daughter will call attention to the need for ministry throughout the church.

In order to move forward and thrive in the rebirth that this painful experience has brought me, I have had to resign myself to the fact that inactivity is not an option. Inactivity is an excuse used by those who are slothful and insensitive to the hurts of others. As deaconesses, if we falter in our duty to be true agents of healing and reconciliation, then one day we will reap the bitter pain of having to face our grandchildren and our guilt-ridden souls and say that in our day of testing we chose inactivity over action. Therefore, I see my life as much more than simply cruising into the senior years "at ease." I heed the clarion call of Isaiah 32:9-11a (NKJV), "Rise up, you women who are at ease; hear my voice, you complacent daughters; give ear

> *As deaconesses, if we falter in our duty to be true agents of healing and reconciliation, then one day we will reap the bitter pain of having to face our grandchildren and our guilt-ridden souls and say that in our day of testing we chose inactivity over action.*

to my speech. In a year and some days you will be troubled, you complacent women; for the vintage will fail, the gathering will not come. Tremble, you women who are at ease; be troubled you complacent ones."

I have found that forgiveness also is not an option. Forgiveness has been fundamental to my healing in order for me to move from a place of pain to a position of power. I pray that if the individual who murdered my precious daughter one cool July night in 2006 confesses to a deaconess, then that deaconess will have more to say than "just pray." I hope that deaconess will share with the individual that true repentance is necessary and Christ is the answer. I pray the deaconess will also explain that Sandra's mother has forgiven him or her and has prayed for his or her soul. I have done so because I refuse to allow the hurting person who hurt my child to continue to hurt me.

Though I will never get over the tragedy of my daughter's death, through a long journey of prayer and introspection, I am finding favor in the sunlight of forgiveness. It has been ironic to experience the life-long empowerment that such a tragic act has blessed me with. The worst has happened and guess what . . . I am still standing! God has allowed the adversary to plunge his dagger into the deepest regions of my soul, yet I still love God! I still worship Him. I still live to glorify Him in my work as a deaconess. Wow! I am amazed myself. God is certainly an awesome God.

Introduction

SPIRITUAL CSI

Through many years of deep reflection and contemplation about my daughter Sandra's untimely death, I have noticed a correlation between her life and mine. In essence, I have performed a spiritual autopsy—a long and methodical search through every page of my life to piece together fragments of deadly words and painful early-life experiences to discover the cause of *my* spiritual death. In the ten years since my daughter's death, like a forensic pathologist, I have examined her life and meticulously compared it to mine. Day-by-day, week by-week, and month-by-month, I have begun to discern the same pattern of painful words left unaddressed and the same toxic methods of masking the pain—and attempting to escape that pain through flight. My flight took me on a vicious, round-trip, 800-mile cycle from Charlotte, North Carolina to Washington, DC. Round and round I went, running from rejection and returning for approval. I went back and forth for nearly 50 years, and it only stopped at the Central Baptist Church in Bladensburg, Maryland, in front of the metallic gold casket of my 46-year-old daughter.

After thorough investigation, my toxicology report revealed to me that it is time for deaconesses to become more insightful, spiritual, and professional if we are going to be effective in ministry in our churches, in general, and with women, in particular. Based upon overwhelming forensic evidence, it has become crystal clear to me that our approach to developing a culture of women with self-worth and wholesome self-esteem must begin far earlier than puberty. My evidence reveals that by the time young women seek out a deaconess for counseling, their souls already have been scarred and their sense of self-worth already marred. Many young women I encounter attempt to mask their hurt behind audacious ambivalence; sarcasm; vulgar, verbally-abrasive words; sexual promiscuity; and an in-your-face, overconfident demeanor. These young women see the world through a much different lens than women who have a solid sense of self. Sadly, their vision of any real future is blurred; their marriages are irreconcilably damaged; and often, their mental, emotional, and spiritual health has been compromised—all because of the unbearable pain they carry within. Essentially, their lives are often in a state of free fall. They live on the edge of life as God has designed. Unknowingly, they walk down the road to ruin, ostentatiously dressed in heavy make-up, high heels, booty shorts, and micro mini-skirts—and displaying BIG ATTITUDE.

It is time for deaconesses to become more insightful, spiritual, and professional if we are going to be effective in ministry.

Deaconesses can no longer be passive or reactive. We must become proactive. Through my greater than 30 years of experience as a deaconess I have found that many people who come through the doors of the church are suffering, unwittingly, from one or both of two deadly wounds—*the father-wound* or *the mother-wound*. One affliction can be deadly, but together, for too many Sandras and Frans, they lead to the same hellacious dead ends—crack houses, abusive men, or worse, a cold, dark tomb. The tomb may be actual, emotional, or metaphoric—but it is just as cold, dark, lonely and frightening. Many church leaders are even unaware of such wounds. However, acknowledging and addressing these wounds as church leaders is critical because they can lead to feelings of anger and abandonment, in addition to other emotional, spiritual, and psychological issues. Such negative feelings often lead souls to dark places, where the brave dare not go.

THE FATHER-WOUND

As a deaconess, I find that many of the women we counsel are suffering from a common culprit, the father-wound. Counseling experts H. Norman Wright[1] and Kathy Rodriguez[2] assert that the father-wound, to a great degree, molds the way we act and react to the men in our lives. Many of us are unaware that nearly every interaction we have with members of the opposite sex is influenced by our father-wound. Our anger toward men, our subconscious distrust of men, and our inability to love our own husbands without serious reservations are often a direct result of our relationship, or lack thereof, with our fathers.

Every day, I see young girls and women who I believe suffer from a father-wound. Their dress and demeanor testify that they are going through life looking for the love that only their fathers can give. This is why I implore every deaconess ministry to work purposefully to help repair the father-wound because the pain of abandonment is so tormenting that no mere general sermon can bring hurting women to the core of its realities.

In my self-reflection, I have come to realize that I, too, am a victim of the father-wound, the acute pain caused by the lack of a strong, loving, and supportive relationship with a responsible father. I, too, have suffered through feelings of abandonment, physically and emotionally, by my father. As a young girl, I did not have the faintest notion that when my father left, and ultimately divorced my mother, he was adversely affecting the rest of my life. It was out of this pain that my attitude toward men was shaped, and my future was set in stone. Unfortunately, there would no deaconess with the dexterity of mind and clarity of mission to guide this young girl through the valley of the shadow of death that I had to travel through in order to reconcile myself with such a deep gash into the fabric of my soul. All that others could see was the outward manifestation of an emptiness that could only be filled with a man by the name of William Moore, my father. My family and community were oblivious that the reason behind my two pregnancies out of wedlock was not that I was a bad girl, but that I had an empty, broken heart. I was not a whore. I was hungry—father hungry[3].

A Closer Look at the Father-Wound

Arguably, the father-wound is by far the most injurious and widespread wound of them all. This is evidenced by the alarming rate of African American youth who grow up without the presence of a father. Overwhelming evidence indicates that girls who grow up with fathers have higher self-esteem, perform better in school, and become more independent. However, girls who grow up without active, caring fathers in their lives go into the adult world with a set of psychological wounds that can create serious struggles in life such as depression, promiscuity, addiction, and controlling behavior.

These detrimental outcomes resulting from the wounds inflicted by earthly fathers make it evident why all children need what Jesus received from His Father at His baptism: "Thou art my beloved Son, in whom I am well pleased" (Mark 1:11). In that one account, we witness:

1. His Father's presence
2. His Father's identification: "My son"
3. His Father"s affection: "My *beloved* son"
4. His Father's approval: "In whom I am well pleased"

With those words of affirmation, Jesus went on to fulfill His purpose to become "the Saviour of the World" (1 John 4:14). God only knows what our children can become with the presence, identification, affection, and approval of their fathers. It is my firm conviction that a caring and devoted father is the most powerful virtuous-woman-making force on the planet. Therefore, it is imperative that the church of the 21st century becomes a father factory.

Jesus said in John 8:32, "Ye shall know the truth and the truth shall make you free." When women afflicted by the father-wound are able to acknowledge the most painful truth of all, "I am a 'daddy-less' daughter,' then healing and restoration can begin. Beyond the pain, is the paradise of freedom: a freedom that is only possible by allowing the love of the great Father of the Universe to embrace all of us with the kind of love that only a divine father can give.

> *My family and community were oblivious that the reason behind my two pregnancies out of wedlock was not that I was a bad girl, but that I had an empty, broken heart. I was not a whore. I was hungry— father hungry.*

THE MOTHER-WOUND

The mother-wound can be found in the intimacy, guidance, and information gap between what we received from our mothers and what we should have received from our mothers. Sadly, many mothers today are unaware of what they should give to their children since they did not receive it themselves. The mother- wound becomes evident as young women physically mature. In days gone by, the wisdom that was imparted from a mother to a child is called "mother-wit[4]." In most cases, mother wit can only be derived from a wise woman of virtue. Young minds are most susceptible to mother-wit during the developmental stages of life. Mother wit is needed to guide adolescent males and females through turbulent situations and toxic relationships. It is not so much biblical, but practical (Although I have discovered that biblical wisdom is extremely practical.). Mother wit teaches young women to judge fairly and think clearly. It creates a critical balance that allows young women to think logically when sexual hormones and testosterone are demanding to take charge.

The lack of mother wit stunts the social and emotional growth of young people. It causes them to approach life lacking hope for the future and distrusting others. Young women tend to expect that all men want is sex and believe that other young women are just competition. The lack of mother wit, in

> *I understand now that the most damaging and injurious words in my own household were the words that were never spoken—the words that were conveyed by shaking heads, mournful grunts, rolling eyes, withheld hugs, and cold, chilling stares.*

many cases, creates vague notions that often push young people into lonely corners of social isolation. In time, the absence of mother-wit creates a warped view of the world and spawns an unhealthy anger toward the mother that did not provide it. From my perspective, the lack of mother-wit is the womb out of which the mother-wound is birthed.

Tragically, I have found that there are many women who carry the title of deaconess who are bleeding profusely from a mother-wound, and these deaconesses, who are charged to aid in the healing of such wounds, are ignorant of the existence of a mother-wound. The prophet Hosea was wise when he wrote, "My people are destroyed for lack of knowledge" (Hosea 4:6 NASB). Therefore, insofar as ministry is concerned, spiritual and emotional healing are basically a hit or miss affair in many churches because leaders are not aware of these lethal wounds from which our young people suffer.

We might also attribute the mother-wound and its effects to the oppression of women within society and in the church, as well. Historically, churches have limited the authority of women within the church and kept women in subjection to men by quoting select passages from Paul's epistles. Even today, the Black church's message of liberation has yet to be fully inclusive insofar as women are concerned. Passages such as "Wives, submit yourselves to your own husbands, as unto the Lord" (Ephesians 5:22) have been taken to include men in general. First Timothy 2:12, "But I suffer not a woman to teach, nor to usurp authority over the man, but to be in silence," has been utilized in many fundamentalist churches to keep well-qualified women in spiritual subservience to less-qualified men. Such primitive views of Scripture cannot help but perpetuate male dominance and abuse in the name of God. This abuse has stirred anger amongst many women, and when angry women raise children—they reproduce their own kind. Anger wounds.

Anger perpetuates anger. Anger kindles a fire that burns until it is extinguished or at the very least managed. Unexpressed or suppressed anger becomes a smothering, venomous caldron that produces vicious scars that mar the soul of its victim. Silence is never the solution to anger, however. Anger must be exposed to the light of God's Word and then released, as we trust God to heal the wounds that anger inflicts. I understand now that the most damaging and injurious words in my own household were the words that were never spoken—the words that were conveyed by shaking heads, mournful grunts, rolling eyes, withheld hugs, and cold, chilling stares.

Evidence of the generational effects of words unspoken can be found by examining the "Silent Generation[5]." The Silent Generation consists of people born approximately between 1925 and 1945. The work ethic this generation modeled is admirable as they worked extremely hard, especially during the Great Depression and World War II. However, they were disciplined to suffer in silence. As a result, most of us who were children of Silent Generation parents did not realize we were poor until we were grown, and our parents did not want us to become "weak," so they often withheld affection from us. They loved their children and desired to protect us from the difficulties in life.

They were determined to give us what they did not get in life. However, they did not give us what they *did* get, nor did they seek to share with us the dark side or underbelly of life. Consequently, our elders hid their disagreements from us, and healthy relationships between women and men were not modeled. As a result, we thought that mama and daddy had the perfect relationship, not knowing they both struggled with anger and were often miserable. Discussions about sexuality also were off the table. Any reference to our private parts was relegated to childish terms such as "wee-wee" or "cherry," and any allusion to the sexual act itself was reduced to such negative connotations as "doing the nasty." Sex was something done in the dark and not to be spoken of publicly. Dad's infidelity was quietly tolerated and, therefore, never talked about. Mama never admitted that she even had sex, let alone enjoyed it. In fact, there are many dirty family secrets that are just coming to light in the face of genetic research and DNA disclosures. Were it not for these technological advances, many of us would have never known that our cousins were really our half-sisters or brothers or that our favorite uncle was really our mother's secret lover.

Discussions about the perils of drugs were also off the table. Yes, daddy had his bottle of gin under the bed or his smoking tobacco or snuff to medicate his pain, but they were never considered drugs. Therefore, we were completely ill-equipped to become parents in a culture that is experiencing a rapid information explosion.

With sex and drug conversations off the table, life—it seems—was off the table since our only vivid remembrances of mama and daddy are of the two of them sitting stoically at the kitchen table or in the front room as if all was well. Certainly, emotions—such as anger, fear and love—were off the table as there was never any real discussion of either. In fact, there was nothing on the table but collard greens, sweet potatoes, ham hocks, and black-eyed peas. So, we just said our grace and dined as if that was all there was to life, and because our parents did not see the world as it was becoming, most of us were ill-equipped and ill-prepared for its overwhelming challenges.

This abbreviated chronicle is not an indictment upon our parents. God bless them: they did the very best they could with what they were given. Rather, recognizing the human flaws of our parents gives us permission to be human, as well. We can acknowledge that we, too, are not perfect, but through Christ, we are being perfected. We can learn from the past and build better relationships with our spouses and children and our extended family.

The most primal fear that humans struggle with is the fear of abandonment. Life began in the comfort and security of our mother's womb, so being alone is foreign to our social nature. For the first nine months, there was always the awareness of a bigger someone there—surrounding us, protecting us, and fulfilling our most basic need, a human presence. Then, we were violently pulled away from that security. It was a traumatic experience, but it was reassuring to be held and cuddled by our mothers and fathers on an almost continual basis. Whenever we momentarily felt disconnected, a loud scream would have them running back and supplying our need for their presence.

Well, what happened when we emitted that loud scream and there was no response? Our response was what researchers call an *attachment disorder.* Ignored cries and calls for help led to us coping the best way we knew how. Attachment disorder varies in degree and type, but I am inclined to believe that many of us struggle with some element of it. As believers, however, we have the comfort of God's promise to be "an ever-present help in trouble" (Psalm 46:1 NIV). In His divine wisdom, our Lord knows our struggles, desires, and our pains. He knows our need for comfort, for relationship. Perhaps this was why the very last words that Jesus spoke to His disciples in Matthew 28:20 were, "I am with you always, even unto the end of the world."

As we read the account of Jesus' final night, we can see clearly that His disciples were troubled by the implication that He would be leaving them. However, the heart of the gospel message is that Jesus will return and receive us unto Himself. As believers, this is the hope that we have, and as deaconesses, this is the hope that we must convey in our ministry. I believe that the goal of the deaconess, in the face of such disorders, is to educate parents and caregivers to its reality.

In his godly wisdom, Solomon exhorted in Proverbs 4:7, "Knowledge is the principle thing so get knowledge, but with all thy getting, get understanding." Where there is no knowledge or understanding in regards to attachment disorder, the cycle will most assuredly continue[6].

Flipping the Script

Instead of judgement and further rejection, it would be worthwhile to consider the following approach to dealing with young women and the mother-wound:

1. Deaconesses meet with the men first to share the importance of a strong father figure in the lives of women. (Before you can aid in the healing of a certain malady, you must identify and understand the root of that malady.)

2. Deaconesses meet with the mother to discuss the mother-wound and share the importance of a spiritually mature mother in the lives of daughters.

3. Deaconesses develop a focused mentoring program. This can be done by each deaconess going into prayer and asking God to reveal to her the young woman in the church in most need of her mentorship. Afterwards, each deaconess needs to devise a deliberate approach to developing a relationship with the young woman God revealed and slowly build that relationship.

4. Once the relationship is developed, that deaconess must commit herself to that relationship, despite difficulty. This develops stability.

5. Each deaconess must resolve not to be judgmental, critical, or nitpick the small things, whereby she will negate her

influence, as the young girl will begin to withdraw. Each deaconess must create an atmosphere of openness (No topic is off limits.). Each deaconess must fasten her seatbelt because the ride will get bumpy, and things that the mentee will share with her may be surprising. Do not be too critical of the mentee's manner of dressing, her language, or her interaction with peers. Make suggestions but not give ultimatums.

6. Develop the discipline to give your advice or express your opinion only when asked. Be patient—in time, she will reach out.

7. Mentors should celebrate each accomplishment, regardless of how small.

8. Over time, you as the mentor should begin to set boundaries and means of accountability. The closer in relationship you get, the more your mentee will seek them.

9. Deaconesses should model the lifestyle that God desires the mentee to aspire.

10. Resist the tendency to pull rank. You are not her mother, nor should you wish to be. You are her mentor to the level of living that she seeks.

Ministering to older women may be a bit more complicated. Their issues are usually tied to toxic relationships that they have developed in search of answers to their pain. They may be in a relationship with an angry, broken female, and they reflect the same negative traits. Often, they are involved with a male who is more of a weight than a wing. In relation to such negativity and toxicity, the book of Jonah gives us great wisdom. In Jonah, we find people in the midst of a severe, life-threatening storm, and the only viable solu- tion is to get Jonah off the ship. It is not until they throw Jonah overboard that the storm begins to desist. We learn here that when we get the wrong people out of our lives, the wrong things will stop happening. By Jonah's own account, he was the problem; therefore, he requested to be thrown overboard. What we fail to destroy on the orders of God will eventually destroy us.

I have often wondered, "Since Jonah knew he was the problem, why didn't he jump overboard to solve the issue?" Like so many people in our lives, he knew he was outside of God's will, yet he did not have the courage to solve the problem. He forced others to deal with his issues. There are people in our lives who know they are a problem. They are operating out of God's will, yet they look to us to do the work. When this is the case, you must take the initiative and throw them off your ship before it sinks with you on it. We must teach young women not to complicate their lives with toxic, unhealthy relationships, but to take control of their own lives and detach from such relationships by any means necessary.

(Un)Planned Parenthood

One of the most life-changing experiences that can happen to a woman is a pregnancy. What happens when that young woman is pregnant and unmarried, and she comes to *you*? How should such a delicate situation be handled? With love.

The utmost care should be given to the child within her body. Prenatal care is essential to give the unborn child an opportunity to live a healthy life. It is for this reason that one of the greatest goals of deaconesses, as relates to young women in crisis, is to share with young women the unconditional love of God that was demonstrated by the sacrificial death of Jesus Christ. This love can best be demonstrated by the unconditional love that deaconesses show toward young women. It may not be an easy task since a lifetime of mother- and father-wounds cannot be healed overnight, but deaconesses must be willing to demonstrate such love persistently.

Young women are accustomed to short term love that is often withdrawn when they demonstrate what the church considers unacceptable, negative, or *ungodly* behavior. Such conditional love is really a counterfeit love that has caused many young women to accept and even expect rejection. It is only when young women experience authentic love that is *in spite of* instead of *because of* that they will begin to open up and embrace the idea that they are worthy of love. When young women experience unconditional love they are better able to give love to their unborn babies and live a lifestyle that is conducive for their unborn fetus—a lifestyle that does not include cigarettes, alcohol, illicit drugs, and stress.

> *We must get beyond the old concept that every young woman who becomes pregnant out of wedlock has the devil in her and beyond the belief that the only answer to every malady that women are stricken with is to pray it out.*

Our mission as deaconesses is clear. If young women are unable to love themselves, then they will be unable to love their children as themselves. If they do not love their children as themselves, then the next generation of young women will experience the same brokenness, and the pain will continue. We must go forward and do the work necessary to make wounded women whole.

THE NEXT CHAPTER

The position of deaconess is not merely a title of honor that is bestowed upon older women in the church in recognition of many years of faithful service. It is far more than that. The stakes are too high, and God's sheep are too precious to simply sit back and celebrate one's successes. God has entrusted and commissioned us as His servants. We must be dutiful and in an unceasing search for what will enrich the lives of those who are suffering the wear and tear of the turbulence that comes with the struggle against an untiring adversary bent on their destruction. Deaconesses should be among the most dedicated, active, and learned of all church leaders because we are charged to minister to the largest group in any church: the female population. It is no hyperbole to say that the future of any church is entrusted to deaconesses. Therefore, deaconesses should be in a continuous mode of developing, becoming, growing, and learning. If one is not up for the task, then perhaps this is the time to move toward the exit because the position of deaconess is one that requires a great zeal for the hurting and a high level of spiritual energy.

In many churches, deaconesses have simply grown too old and too tired. The deaconesses in our churches need to get younger. Not necessarily younger in age (although this is true in most churches), but younger in energy and thinking. In order to minister effectively in this new and challenging 21st century, we must be flexible and open to new and innovative methods of tackling the complex issues with which women are confronted. Some remark that the greatest obstacle in most churches is old people, and I must agree. The church does not need any more old people, but the church is in desperate need of elders.

If deaconesses are going to minister effectively in this new century, then we must get beyond the old concept that every young woman who becomes pregnant out of wedlock has *the devil in her* and beyond the belief that the only answer to every malady that women are stricken with is to *pray it out*. Though

I am old school and believe that the devil is, in some form, the root cause of most of what young women struggle with—I also believe in the power of prayer because I am a product of its power. However, too often deaconesses and other church leaders use the devil and prayer as easy outs and means by which to avoid the hard work that it takes to truly empower and deliver souls who have been victimized by hurting men, sexist systems, and a world that preys upon the old and defenseless as well as the young and naive. It is with this in mind that I beckon deaconesses to a more professional approach to ministry so that we will stop blaming the victims for a crime that has been perpetrated against them, while allowing the real culprits to go scot-free. We must become as efficient in our work as crime scene investigators, pulling back the layers, searching for clues, analyzing evidence, drawing conclusions, and bringing closure and healing to families. Then, and only then, will the church cease shooting our wounded and destroying our seed.

I want readers of this text to understand fully the significance of having a committed, effective deaconess in one's life, and the detriment that befalls too many young women when they do not. Therefore, I begin this book by exploring my story and exposing the hurts and hurdles in journey in hopes that Frans and Sandras across our communities might be better understood and assisted in our churches. In Section III, I address more specifically "How a Deaconess Can Make a Difference." How could a deaconess have made a difference in my trouble-filled life? How much different might my life have been if I would have had an effective deaconess? Perhaps much of the pain that required an effective deaconess would not have been necessary if I would have had a father and mother who were aware of how their irresponsible actions could impact my life. If the deaconesses in my church would have been cognizant of the wounds from which I was suffering, then maybe their approach to ministering to me would have gone further than the time-worn phrase of *you need prayer.* While I certainly am not discounting the power of prayer, I am suggesting that prayer is a unilateral approach to a multilateral problem that goes deeper, far deeper, than anyone could imagine. As deaconesses, we must be prepared to effectively serve communion, but we must also be equipped and committed to serving our communities.

Section I

THE MAKING OF A DEACONESS: MY JOURNEY

Through many dangers, toils and snares,
I have already come;
'Tis grace that bro't me safe thus far,
And grace will lead me home.

"Amazing Grace"

IN THE BEGINNING . . .

I was a carefree little girl. I was raised in a four-family duplex in Charlotte, North Carolina. Like most poor black children in urban Charlotte in the 1950's, I was nurtured with high morals and family values. My grandmother, whom I affectionately called "Mama," was the backbone of the household—although both my mother and father lived in the same dwelling.

I have fond memories of my early childhood, memories of playing baseball in the backyard with the boys in my extended family. When there was no baseball, I gladly volunteered my dolls. However, when my daddy showed up he would scold the boys for using the dolls I had relinquished for baseball duty. He never included me in the scolding, even though I was a willing participant. Though I was what some would call a tomboy, I was also daddy's little girl.

On Sundays, my younger brother Eddie and I were compelled to attend the Little Rock A. M. E. Church. We seldom missed church since it was on the same block where we lived. Church time was often a continuation of playtime. That is, until Mama gave us what we called *the look*. Everybody in church knew the look that said, "If you children don't be quiet and pay attention, you will surely suffer the consequences."

After church, we would all enjoy Sunday dinner together and later gather around the radio to listen to gospel music or comedy shows—if we didn't have a Sunday evening service or Buds of Promise youth group meeting.

My early childhood was fairly idyllic. Days were carefree and nights were restful. I slept with Mama because she said I kept her back warm. One tragic morning, however, my idyllic childhood was shattered. On that dreadful day, I was abruptly awakened by my Uncle John and taken upstairs. I soon learned that sometime during the night my precious Mama had died. I am haunted to this day as I am not sure just how long I had lain in the bed with my dead grandmother! I guess I didn't do a very good job keeping her back warm.

My daddy began to drink heavily, which triggered frequent arguments with my mother. Daddy contended they were becoming "incompatible" because they did not drink together. Eventually, Daddy moved out, and we began to move from place to place. My mother became the breadwinner, and I believe the stress caused her to take daddy's place as the family alcoholic. My daddy never returned, and he eventually divorced us. A decade later, I found myself on a train heading north to Washington, DC, with 24 dollars in my purse, two "born out of wedlock" little girls under my arms, and pain in my heart, listening to the clack-a-de-clack of those steel railroad wheels—moving hastily toward an uncertain future. My name is Frances Jones, and *The Making of a Deaconess* is my story.

THE FLIGHT

As I hurriedly boarded the train for Washington, DC in the fall of 1964 with my two daughters, Sandra and Tina, I did so with great fear and apprehension. Quietly, I sat in that rather crowded passenger car wondering what awaited me in our nation's capital. Shamefully, I pondered my embarrassing predicament: unmarried, two infant daughters to raise, and two 10's, three 1's, three quarters, two dimes, and one nickel to my name. As that noisy locomotive raced down that bumpy track, I wondered just how daddy's little girl could have gotten herself into such a mess. And then there was the unsettling prospect of what mama would think when she arrived back home in Charlotte to find her daughter and two grandchildren gone—running from a scandalous past and racing toward an uncertain future.

My heart began to pound within my chest as I thought of her opening that rickety wooden door, calling our names, and hearing nothing but dead silence. Closets empty, chest of drawers bare, and only a half-empty carton of milk in the fridge. I imagine the feeling of abandonment probably caused her to curse my existence and drink the night away. I didn't leave a note. What was there to say? I had cleared out and taken Sandra and Tina with me. As much as I wanted to share with her what I was planning to do, I knew that if I had, she would have talked me out of it. So, there I was, heading north, hopefully—prayerfully—to make a decent home for my two babies.

As I pondered my fate, from time to time, I had to quiet either Sandra or Tina. They were two and one year old, respectively, at the time. Sitting in that lonely railroad car, thoughts flashed through my mind like lightning bolts. I thought about their father, who was never really a daddy—not that I had really been a mother. I wondered how my life had been transformed so quickly from the warmth and stolen moments of intimacy with Charles in my mother's bed to the loneliness and alienation of this chilly boxcar moving swiftly through the dark of night. *How could I have let him, or even my daddy, convince me he loved me? I should have known he was no good the first time around.* Over and over, I could hear my mother's voice echoing through the corridors of my pathetic soul, "It was bad enough making one mistake, but two!" But as Tina lay in my lap and Sandra slept against my shoulder, I silently prayed, "Lord, how could I ever refer to my beautiful babies as mistakes?" I desperately wanted to burst forth with tears, but I had to stay strong for my children's sake.

I reached into my purse again to examine my cash flow. *Still only 24 dollars*, as if I were expecting it to earn interest in my purse. Even so, there was no reason to worry—at least about a place to stay—since my homegirl Bobbie Jean promised there would be plenty of room in the house her mother Nannie rented in DC. With 24 dollars and a roof over our heads, we would be just fine, I tried to convince myself. I had heard jobs were plentiful in DC, so I figured I would be working in no time, perhaps even able to send mama something.

My mama, Big Frances, was a proud woman who, along with my aunts, never let me forget that I would never amount to anything. She made clear that she was hurt and embarrassed by her tall, top-heavy, lanky, and often awkward daughter who did not have sense enough not to get pregnant TWICE by the same "no good nigg**" (to use her rather trenchant words). Mama worked at Ivey's department store earning approximately 17 dollars a week and made sure her children were in church every Sunday. She wanted nothing but the best for my younger brother Eddie and me, but she never really explained how not to get pregnant, except for not sitting in a boy's lap and not kissing. I don't do much kissing, even today, I imagine because kissing got me into so much trouble as a teenager.

I was so naïve, in fact, that I did not realize that I was in the family way with Sandra until my uncle Arthur, rather abruptly, raised the possibility one evening after observing me vomit repeatedly. *No way*, I convinced myself, because my girlfriend Annie Laura had assured me that I could not get knocked up as long as I drank ginger or sat in some mustard either before or after being with a boy. After it was confirmed that I was indeed with child, tension between my mother and me, which always seemed to exist, increased. There were times when I honestly wondered if mama even liked me, let alone loved me. I knew she did, but nevertheless, I wondered.

On the other hand, I took comfort in knowing I was daddy's little girl. It was consoling to think of the times I spent with my daddy, William. Daddies give daughters intangible and much-needed validation. I felt so secure being in my daddy's arms. In retrospect, I know now that I was looking for my daddy's love when my children were conceived. Looking back, I believe that if daddy and mama had stayed together, or at least daddy had been more active during my adolescence—a critical time in my life—I would have been in my junior year at somebody's college instead of on a train headed to a city that scared me to death—with two children at my side, no wedding ring on my finger, and only 2 tens, 3 ones, and a dollar's worth of change in my patent leather purse.

RUDE AWAKENING

Arriving in Washington, I discovered that the big house I was looking forward to was a one-bedroom apartment, which had to be shared with five adults and a two-year old child. Including my two daughters and me, there were nine individuals in that cramped one-bedroom apartment. Talk about disillusionment! The very thought of such an arrangement gives a new definition to the word.

Soon after my arrival, I secured employment at Eddie Leonard's Sandwich Shoppe, a local fast food restaurant, where I earned 80 dollars a week, plus tips. However, I had to work the night shift, 8 p.m. to 4 a.m. Fortunately, the restaurant paid for a cab ride home, so I didn't have too much room to complain. I endured the uncomfortable arrangement of nine people living in a one-bedroom apartment for nine months until Nannie, the housemother, rented a fairly decent house in upper Northwest. This house afforded us a lot more privacy, and for the first time in nearly a year in a new city, we began to feel like residents—instead of sardines.

While working at the sandwich shoppe, I met a young woman named Belle. We became close friends, and eventually, the girls and I moved into Belle's one-room bungalow. This arrangement lasted until Belle informed me that some "out-of-town" relative was coming to live with her. Implicit in her notice of the relative en route was the fact that I had to uproot my children once again.

About that time, I met a young woman around my age named Mary. So, it was goodbye Belle and hello Mary. I am sure the girls were wondering if we would ever really settle down in one place for more than a few months.

The girls and I really enjoyed living with Mary. I would get up each morning and prepare breakfast for Mary and the girls, and for a while, things could not have been better. Then one day, I became ill with strep throat and decided to stay in bed. My feelings were crushed when I overhead Mary complaining to a friend how I was leisurely lying around the place like I was somebody special. I was sick for God's sake! This angered and hurt me so much that I decided to leave. It was then that I remembered a neighbor back home telling me about her brother in Washington who would help me if I needed it. I decided to look him up. His name was Fred Hall, and I did not know at that time that he would become more than just a Washington source of benevolence. I explained my situation to him, and he immediately made his nicely furnished apartment available to my girls and me. He explained that he was seldom at home and would appreciate having someone to serve as a caretaker over the place. Eventually, with just a little Ajax cleanser and a feminine touch, I transformed his quaint and shabby bachelor's apartment into a cozy home for my babies.

REGRETFUL RETURN

Fred Hall was a small-framed man with a big and caring heart. He and I became the best of friends. He would stop by from time to time to check on the girls and me. Although he had a propensity to over-indulge in alcohol, we enjoyed his company when he was around. The times when all of us could be together were fun for the girls and rather enjoyable for me. Things could not have been better. That is, until I returned home one morning and found Tina, my youngest daughter, sitting in the middle of the floor playing with a broken glass while my dollar-a-day babysitter was completely drunk. Right then and there, I decided I would return home. The price of the safety of my children was too much to pay for our independence.

So, I swallowed my pride, which almost strangled me, quit my job, packed up Sandra and Tina, and returned to dreaded Charlotte within the week. I cannot begin to express how it felt returning to my mother's house, especially in light of the way I left. Nor can I express the despair and hopelessness I carried in my bosom having to return home like a whipped hound dog with his tail between his legs. That had to be one of the darkest moments of my life.

Soon after I returned, my mother and Aunt Alice (whom we affectionately called "Weasel") suggested I leave the girls in Charlotte and return to Washington. They assured me they would take good care of my "chil'rins," and I assured them I would send money regularly and visit as often as possible. But even with the joy of having the opportunity to return to Washington, where I was sure I could make a better future for my daughters, I cannot fully articulate my reluctance and the feelings of guilt surrounding the prospect of leaving my girls. In retrospect, I regret that decision, although I do not know how I could have fully grown up if I had stayed in Charlotte.

After two weeks in Charlotte, I reluctantly returned to Washington and to the apartment of Fred Hall. Having quit my job to return to Charlotte, I was back in the big city unemployed. Fred, however, secured employment for me at Frito Lay, where I was making 100 dollars a week. One week, after taxes, I even brought home a whopping 120 dollars. Talk about living the good life. Yours truly was finally making it in the nation's capital. I sent a fair amount of money home and visited on many weekends and most holidays. Whenever I visited, I would bring gifts for my girls, my mother, and my aunts and uncles. It was Christmas every time I went home. It felt so good being able to give gifts to those who never thought I would amount to anything.

In a sense, I guess I was trying to somehow purchase my self-respect by giving to those who had such a negative impact on my sense of self-worth. I could see the surprise, almost envy, in their eyes as I handed them the installment payments on the love I so badly needed from my family. But it seemed like the more I gave, the more sinister and sarcastic they became. There were times when I could not wait to leave Charlotte and return to the serenity of Fred Hall's apartment. I truly enjoyed the solitude of what was rapidly becoming my refuge, and Fred enjoyed having his apartment occupied while he lived the free-wheeling life of a bachelor.

Over time, our friendship developed into much more, principally on the part of Fred. In my heart of hearts, I knew I really did not love him, or shall I say I was not in love with him, but we both agreed we ought to marry. For the life of me, I have no idea where my head was at the time, but we married and set up house.

The Great Escape

Fred and I lived together for over four years, and over those four years, the little drinking habit that I observed as a friend became intolerable as a wife. As the years rolled by, I knew there was something more to life than being married to a man who was also married to cheap Scotch. One evening, I suggested that we separate. He adamantly opposed and became abusive at the very idea, so much so that he locked me in our bedroom. That one act sealed our fate. I was determined that no one, and I mean no one, would treat me that way. Like a caged animal, I longed to be free. Almost instinctively, I bailed out through the bedroom window and ran to freedom. With that, the Fred Hall chapter in my life was marked *finished*!

After the great escape from Fred in 1970, I returned to Nannie's house of refuge where things had not gotten any better as far as space was concerned. The house was slightly larger, but the number of tenants had grown to 14. I shared a room with my friend Bobbie Jean. Realizing that the only way out of this musical house cycle was to work my way out, I immersed myself in pursuit of the almighty dollar. I secured employment as a waitress at the Army-Navy Country Club in Arlington, Virginia. Very soon, I became a barmaid, a female bartender. It was then that I began to heavily partake of the drinks I mixed: Singapore slings, salty dogs, and rusty nails were just a few of the potions. I would mix drinks for the elite patrons of the country club who made drinking fashionable, and thereby acceptable to me.

Drinking became a way to numb the pain that I felt deep within. When I drank, I would forget negative and ominous assessments of my family insofar as women who bore children out of wedlock were concerned. Alcohol was a way of drowning out the words that seemed to echo in my head—mean, nasty, and ugly words that repeatedly posed the rhetorical question of who would really want a woman with two kids born as "bastards." Without a cocktail, I could not cope with the fact that I was damaged goods. My heart ached for someone to make me feel that I had worth beyond foolish fornication and sordid circumstances. My soul screamed in the night for some kind of redemption, but there was nothing and no one to guide me through the maze of malicious thoughts that seemed to validate my negative assessment of self. With the exception of my daddy, no man could see beyond the size of my breasts or the shape of my rear end. As far as men were concerned, they were all named Charles, and they all caused pain.

There were times, however, when I thought I should have married my daughters' daddy Charles. This would have at least made mama happy and my children "legitimate." We attempted to get married once or twice, but thank God, I was under age and could not do so without my parent's signature. Marriage might have solved the immediate dilemma but would have done very little to boost my sense of self-esteem. I needed someone to marry me for me, not my pitiful and pathetic condition.

PRISON WITH NO BARS

After several months of working at the country club, I was

finally able to get my own place. I applied, not really expecting I would qualify for my own apartment, and low and behold, I was approved. I was so excited that I would finally be able to move away from the crowded condition of Nannie's to my own place. There was only one small problem: I had no furniture and no means of purchasing even a bed. However, I was determined, so I borrowed a bed from my friend Bobbie Jean and moved in. Talk about free at last! Thank God Almighty, I was free at last! That freedom, however, was only on the exterior. Inwardly, I was a miserable wretch. Inwardly, I was still a prisoner of a painful past, and no amount of money could buy my freedom. No living arrangement, be it a crowded house or a luxuriously furnished apartment, could fill the emptiness of my soul. I found myself in an endless cycle of parties weekend after weekend, by myself, searching for love in all the wrong places—only to return home escorted by loneliness and despair. I knew in my heart this cycle would have to end, but for the life of me, I did not know how to end it.

In May of 1974, Aunt Alice (Weasel) passed away. She, along with my mother, was caring for my daughters in Charlotte. When I attended the funeral and saw the condition of my mother, I knew I would be bringing my children, who were teenagers by then, back to Washington with me. My mother had begun to drink heavily and incessantly, and I could not chance the safety of my girls with her, as if I were much better. All I could think about was the fact that I did not want my daughters to go through the pain I had endured at the hands of my mother. Mama, when she was not drinking, was extremely negative, but she was tolerable. However, she was a terror on two feet when she was drinking. So, I was off to Washington again with my two daughters, running from my mama.

When I returned to Washington with my teenaged daughters, I increased my work routine. Sometimes working two or three jobs, I was determined to provide for my children and numb the pain within my soul. However, it seemed like the frightening footsteps of my past were getting louder and louder, and I became an emotional wreck. There were times when I felt like I was losing my mind, and I didn't know why. One day, I remembered my grandmother had advised me that if I ever truly needed help, I should, "Turn to the Lord and pray." One Saturday night, driving home from *another* party, I started to cry. Eventually, I cried out to God saying, "Lord, please help me. Please help me." Nannie would always invite me to her church, but somehow, I would never find my way. The next morning, I got up, dressed the girls, and went to church. As I approached the doors of the church, I did not know what to expect, but I knew I wanted to escape a life wrought with emptiness, pain, and despair.

When I exited the doors of the Mt. Carmel Freewill Baptist Church that Sunday afternoon, I was feeling good. The service seemed just what I needed. Emotions were high, and the fellowship of that small but close congregation made me feel encouraged. I felt a sense of love and acceptance. I shall never forget Bishop Robert Gillespie and the Mt. Carmel family for giving me what I needed that Sunday. For the first time, it did not seem to matter that I was a *loose woman*. I felt worth something even though I was damaged goods, as my family in Charlotte depicted me. I felt the love I needed—the love I had tried to purchase when I would return home to Charlotte with an arm full of gifts. It is strange how we try to buy love by giving to those who never seem to accept us. Well, on that Sunday, I received something that I needed so desperately. I received love, and boy, did it feel wonderful.

I officially became a part of the Mt. Carmel church family in September of 1976. My lifestyle did not change to any great degree, but I felt better about myself. There was still an itch in my life that was not getting scratched, but as I attended church service each Sunday, at least I did not have the hives I had prior to that first Sunday. Before long, however, the ache and emptiness that initially compelled me to attend church slowly began to creep back. This time, however, it was accompanied by guilt—the guilt of living contrary to the preaching I was hearing on Sunday morning. The guilt of coming to church hearing the preacher talk about how Christians ought not party, drink, engage in fornication, or use profanity—knowing that I was guilty of all the above. It seems back then that churches were big on telling people *what* to do but gave very little instruction to its members in the area of *how*.

Thus, I could tell you in my sleep *what* I ought to do, but I could not begin to explain in my most spiritual state *how* to do what I knew I *ought* to do. Yes, resist temptation, but *how* was the issue I wrestled with. Therefore, my presence in the worship service, as time rolled by, became less and less the emotional release I had experienced on that first Sunday. Hence, my time in worship service became more and more a time of torment—three hours of internal turmoil as I was eaten like a cancer with guilt.

Eventually, my attendance became sporadic, needless to say to the delight of my teenage girls. However, I never abandoned church altogether since I felt it was my duty to keep my daughters in church. From time to time, I would even attend Tuesday night prayer service. I did so in hopes that I would be able to receive what I perceived the older, seasoned, victorious saints had received. When I sat in church and saw the faith that illuminated from their faces, heard the power in their testimonies, and witnessed the strength they displayed in the spirit realm, I hungered for what they seemed to possess. I could see that I needed much more than the feel-good emotion I had experienced on that initial Sunday. So, I set about my quest for that *something more* by attending prayer service.

Before long, it happened. I experienced a breakthrough. That breakthrough was preceded by an amplified period of pain. When I would attend church and prayer service, over and over again I would hear about the love of Jesus, but I had not experienced that love. In fact, in my heart I was wondering how in the world could Jesus, as high and holy as He is, love someone as lowly as me. I could not, in a thousand years, fathom love from One so divine. At the same time, I knew I needed His love. I needed it so badly that I ached for it.

From the outside, it may have seemed like I was living the life. I had moved into my own townhouse. For the first time in my life, I had my own bedroom, and I had my own transportation, a 1972 Ford Grand Torino. If someone would had told me when I first arrived in Washington that I would have progressed to this point in my life, I would have thought he or she was insane. When I arrived in the nation's capital a decade earlier, attaining such an opulent lifestyle was my ideal, but in reality, while in my townhouse, my own bedroom, and driving my new used car—I ached for love. I ached for someone to love me for me. Not because of my figure, but my person. Not because I would give gifts or send money and not because I was mommie or sweetheart—but because I was me.

Thanks be to God, four years after joining the church, on April 12, 1980, my search came to an end. I found that someone. At prayer service that evening, I asked the Lord to come into my life, and He did. As He did, for the first time since my daddy last held me in his arms, I felt love. Unconditional love. And with that love came a peace, truly, a peace that passed all understanding. And even with the almost endless storms that accompanied raising children in a big city, I knew the love I had found would prevail. So on that fateful evening at Mt. Carmel Freewill Baptist Church, I knew I had finally turned the corner because the pain I had felt every day since I discovered I was pregnant, nearly 16 years earlier, had finally begun to subside.

My Angels, My Anguish

My daughters were always the anchors for my life. In many ways, they were my single source of love and joy. After all, for so long, they were all I really had. From their births, they were my motivation for getting up each morning, my incentive for going to work, and my reason for seeking a life greater than what I experienced in Charlotte. For so long, in my mind at least, my daughters were my reason for existence. Were it not for my two little girls, I would have had no reason to go on, no reason to endure the pain of Charlotte, North Carolina, or the early days in Washington, DC, and no reason to improve my lot in life.

My daughters were often the single, motivating factor in my BC (Before Christ) days. I shudder to think where I would be or what I would have done were it not for the fact I had two little lives that needed me. Without them, I would have had no incentive to get a better job or to seek a better place to live. Somehow, what I once received from my father, longed for from my mother, and desperately sought from men in my life was—to some extent—fulfilled when I held and cuddled Sandra and Tina. It seems that Sandra and Tina were what gave me real worth. The moment they cried into this world they dominated my thoughts, my daily schedule, my budget, my being, and my life. They brought such unimaginable joy that I suppose it was only natural they bring an equal amount of excruciating pain.

Salvation Was Not Insulation

Gradually, I learned that salvation in Christ does not mean insulation from the trials that come with life. As the pain of not feeling loved subsided, because of my relationship with Christ, the pain and challenges of being a mother in our sin-sick society began to invade my being. Initially, it began as the normal turmoil of parenting teenagers. Sandra and Tina had lived an almost gypsy lifestyle ever since we made the first trip to Washington. Since the time of our initial arrival in our nation's capital, they had been shuttled from Nannie's one bedroom to Belle's efficiency, to Mary's apartment, to Fred Hall's bachelor flat, to Charlotte with my mother and aunt, and back to Washington with me again. I often wondered what lasting effects the constant displacement and relocation would have on their overall development and maturity. Common sense said that living such a transitory existence would not have a positive impact, but I hoped the negatives would not be permanent.

One of the negatives that I learned about, after they were grown, was that they were subjected to a barrage of "anti-Frances propaganda" while living with my mother in Charlotte. I cannot fully express the level of anger that seized my soul when I was made aware of such Frances bashing. It pained me to think that while I was in Washington, working my behind off and sending every dollar I could muster back to Charlotte for the care of my daughters, they were hearing things about their mother that were not very flattering, to say the least. I wish I had known at the time about the torrent of terrible tidbits my daughters were subjected to in my absence. It devastated me to learn of this, and I cannot fathom what impact the words of scornful relatives, and even my own mother, had on my two babies.

Around the time that I found peace with God, my eldest daughter Sandra began keeping company with a rambunctious crowd at school and in our neighborhood. I do not know the extent of her peers' influence, but I do know she began to display behavior that was far different from what I had attempted to instill in her. She did poorly in school, and as time passed, she neglected school altogether. She also began to act out at home, which was a source of great agony, and the resulting stress cast a dark cloud of depression over our entire household. The more I warned, and even whipped, the more rebellious she became. After a while, she began to stay out late at night. The sleepless nights began to rob me of my spiritual joy. My prayers became hollow, my praise became empty, and my walk with Christ became a weary stroll through the darkest of nights. I wondered how things could get any worse, but eventually, my worst nightmare became reality. My beloved Sandra became afflicted with an addiction to drugs.

During the almost two-decade pursuit of Sandra's deliverance, I discovered I was also pursuing my own deliverance and spiritual healing. It was during this agonizing pursuit that I began to understand the distinction between salvation, deliverance, and healing. Naively, I had assumed that when I received Christ as Savior on April 12, 1980, I also received complete deliverance and healing from the wounds of my past. Quite the contrary, the deliverance and healing process *began* on April 12, 1980, and the healing journey has been ongoing and continues today. I see now what I could not see in 1964. I see that my critical and scornful attitude toward my family in Charlotte, and sometimes Sandra, were unhelpful for them and unhealthy for me. I realize that running from the pain was unproductive unless I was running toward and into the arms of the Lord.

Throughout Sandra's years of struggling, I used to wonder why I could not let go of her, but God revealed to me that in Sandra Yvette, I saw myself, Frances Anne. Sandra Yvette was merely a mirror image of Frances Anne. In Sandra, I relived the pain and horror that I experienced in my life. For all those years, in attempting to save Sandra, I was actually attempting to save Frances. I saw in *her* deliverance *my* deliverance from the past, not deliverance *to* the future. Perhaps that is why I ran throughout the city putting myself in danger trying to rescue her. I identified with Sandra's pain, for like Sandra, I attempted to run away from the hurt, the rejection, and the alienation when I left Charlotte all those years ago. In Sandra's attempt to escape her pain by getting high on illicit drugs, I saw my need to escape the painful words of my mother and aunts by turning to alcohol. In Sandra's tendency to be abused and used by men, I saw my own tendency to be abused and used by the Charles' of the world. In Sandra's need to purchase the love and acceptance of others, I saw my need to do likewise. In my precious daughter Sandra's bumpy journey toward what seemed like the Land of Oz—wholeness—I see my own long sojourn toward wholeness.

> *In attempting to save Sandra, I was actually attempting to save Frances. I saw in her deliverance my deliverance from the past, not deliverance to the future.*

SALVATION'S TURBULENT EPILOGUE

Little did I know there was so much pain associated with God's love. In the years that have bridged 1980 to the present, I have grown to appreciate the awesome pain the Savior had to endure to secure our salvation. I have also come to appreciate the excruciating pain our Lord continues to endure for our ongoing sanctification. I, too, have suffered. For over three decades now, since the dawn of my salvation that blessed evening at Mt. Carmel, I have been forced to endure what has often seemed like an endless, nightmarish roller coaster ride of emotional anguish.

After the initial glow of my salvation began to fad and the reality of my painful state began to raise its ugly head, I had to fight tooth and nail for Sandra's deliverance from the hellish, fiendish clutches of drug addiction. That fight continues, even today, because my pain only intensified with her passing. The moment when I received the call of her murder was unforgettable. When my younger daughter called me with the news, it was about 10:15 on a Monday night. Like it was yesterday, I remember falling on my face. I was inconsolable as I wept gallons of tears of sorrow and regret.

I can relate well to Paul's suffering that he describes in Chapter 12 of his second letter to the church at Corinth. Paul writes that his "thorn in the flesh" was allowed to be there to "buffet him," to keep him humble and from being "exulted above measure" (v. 7). For two decades, my daughter's drug addiction served as my thorn in the flesh. Not Sandra, but her drug addiction was the source of my great affliction. I make this distinction because when my daughter's life was taken on July 10, 2006, there was no joy, no feeling of relief, no weight lifted. The thorn was not removed. If I could bring my daughter back with the struggle of drug addiction, I would do so in a heartbeat.

Since Sandra's passing, I have learned to separate the illness from its victim. I have also learned that Sandra's real problem was not drug addiction; drugs were only a means by which she sought to cope with her undiagnosed bipolar condition. *The thorn* and my daughter were not the same, and I know now that the anguish of our struggle was not drug addiction but her bipolar condition, which went undiagnosed most of her life. Though drug addiction was her affliction, Sandra did not die from a drug overdose. She was murdered. Murdered at a time when she had been clean for several months and had even become a licensed minister. Her initial sermon focused on being delivered from the crack rock to the solid rock of Jesus. I will never forget the pride I experienced on the occasion of her entrance into ministry. Though the struggle was great, I will always remember how valiantly she fought her addiction, not knowing that she was fighting the wrong illness with the wrong weapon.

My post-salvation, spiritual and emotional roller-coaster ride is best depicted by a journal entry I wrote while still in the midst of the storm. Though my days of worry about her safety and salvation have passed, this segment of my experience is a reminder of my ongoing victory. I call this entry, "Nocturnal Agony."

10:00	I love Sandra... I loathe Sandra. I wish she'd call... I wouldn't care if I never heard from her again.
10:10	Oh God... my child is out there somewhere...please take care of my child. When will this nightmare end... probably not until she's dead. At least I'd know where to find her!
10:17	Oh God once and for alL .. bring this hellish dream to an end.
10:20	RING PHONE! RING! Be Sandra... be the morgue!
10:40	Oh Lord forgive me for thinking that! !! But that's how I feel.
11:00	I can't sleep...1 must go out and search for her. Oh no...I'm not going anywhere... I'm tired of running behind Sandra as she chases a high.
11:03	But she's my child... she's probably cold. Shoot she's probably feeling better than me... she's probably feeling no pain.
11:13	I should at least drive over at Nannie's house. I think I'll just call. But suppose she isn't... then Nannie would know... and I don't want Nannie to know.
11:30	What time is it now? 11:30 just three minutes from the last time I looked. This is ridiculous I'm going to bed. For what? I can't sleep.
11:50	I'll call Pastor...just to talk maybe he's heard something. Oh no, it's too late. Or is it, well, yes it is.
12:15	Where are my so-called friends when I really need them? Oh that's not fair.
12:30	Oh, the phone is ringing, "Hello... Sandra where are you? Can you come by, can you spend the night? Look girl, I'm tired of fooling with you!!! Yeah, come on. I love you too, bye."
12:34	Oh girl, I hate you.
	(Four hours later)
3:30	I wonder what happened. It's 3:30. No Sandra. Wherever you are. Stay there! I hope I don't ever see you again!
3:43	Maybe I was too harsh.
4:00	Lord, where is my child?
4:10	Sandra, I love you. I loathe you.
4:27	Sandra, I love you. I loathe you.
4:34	Sandra, I love you. I loathe you.
4:47	Sandra, I love you. I loathe you.
4:52	Sandra, I love you. I loathe you.
5:00	I'm so tired! So tired!! Tired of this roller coaster ride.

My regret is my impetus for this publication. As a deaconess, I was completely ignorant to what was going on in my daughter's life that drove her to seek relief through drugs. All too often, deaconesses in the church are ill-equipped to minister to the real needs of women. Our default answer of "pray about it" is perhaps the reason why women do not find the church relevant in today's society. In many cases, the issues women face today are simply too complex for today's deaconesses. The plethora of problems that afflict young women today demand deaconesses and ministers who are serious and sincere about lifting fallen humanity. When Paul advises us to study to show ourselves approved, he means more than merely attending Sunday school, wearing white, serving communion, and sitting piously in the church looking down our noses at the people we are supposed to be serving. If we are ever to hear the voice of our Savior say, "Well done," then we must be good and faithful servants and not pompous, judgmental, self-righteous busybodies. We need spiritual discernment and a means to respond to what is revealed through prayer and observation.

My daughter is with the Lord today because, in many ways, she was abandoned by those whom God had placed on earth to help her through the dark nights of her depression and frustration. This is why I vow to never give up on another young woman who struggles with issues that make her vulnerable to the streets.

THE MORNING BREAKS

Today, as I look back over the chasm of time God gave Sandra and me together on this planet, I celebrate her life, a life of innocence, naiveté, laughter, joy, and a sincere desire to serve the Lord. Her legacy is two beautiful children and a grandmother who loves them dearly.

And now, sitting in the springtime of my own deliverance, I am encouraged, blessed, and inspired to continue to work toward ultimate deliverance of so many other Sandras wandering aimlessly in this world with no one who truly understands what they are going through. If you are a Sandra, and you are reading these words, I encourage to you never give up, to never give in. There is an answer to what you are going through and how you are feeling. The answer begins with your knowing that God's grace is sufficient for you. I was poor, brokenhearted, captive, blind, and bruised, but now, when I look into the mirror, I see the Lord staring back at me saying, "By my stripes, you are healed." So today, in my deliverance and healing, I go forth speaking the words of Jesus: "The Spirit of the Lord is upon me, for he has anointed me to bring Good News to the poor. He has sent me to proclaim that captives will be released, that the blind will see, that the oppressed will be set free" (Luke 4:18, NLT).

When you are tempted to become victim of the frightful scare tactics of the adversary, remember God's grace. It is often heard in the church, "Oh, what peace we often forfeit; oh, what needless pains we bear, all because we do not carry everything to God in prayer."[7] Oh, how I wish I had taken that song to heart—not just hearing, but listening. For almost 20 years I anguished, forfeiting much-needed peace, bearing uncertain pain. I thank God that I can say with all that is within me that the long night of my suffering has given way to the dawn of a brand new day.

My poem, "Morning Reflections," expresses my journey of healing as I continue to love, grow, forgive, and live.

Morning Reflections:
Living in the Wake of Nocturnal Agony

As I awaken from nocturnal agony, I think of the times we spent in maternal ecstasy.

The long night of despair has ended, and today, I see you in the light of the glistening, shimmering sunlight of dawn's early light.

I see you anew, not as you lay in eternal slumber, but as you were in the early days of laughter.

My nocturnal loathing has been transformed into a divine longing.
A longing that will only be satisfied when we meet again on the distant shores of heaven's soothing seas.

But as we spend these days that we are physically apart, my precious Sandra, I need you to know just how much you are missed.

I hear your voice in the whispering wind, I see your face in the daughter you entrusted me to guide, and in the son that has grown so tall.

I sense your presence in every sanctuary song that echoes in worship. I especially hear your "out of tune" voice singing your favorite hymn "Love Lifted Me."

That hymn so reminds me that you are ever so near, and it lifts me with joyous reminders of moments we spent together. I all but hear your heartbeat as I sit quietly and remember.

The nocturnal agony has given way to a brand new day, and the love we shared on earth returns every time I hear a girl-child call out and her ma reaches for her tender, gentle hand.

Surely Sandra, my mourning has turned into dancing as thoughts of you return each day that I live and love and long to see your smiling face or your warm embrace.

Yes Sandra, the dark days have given way to the hope that

accompanies the faith that you taught me and I seek to give others.

So, I thank you, my eldest daughter, for every memory that is ours alone, and I know that you are home with the One you so longed to see.

And one day, I know in my heart that you and I, Big Frances, my beloved William, and maybe even Aunt Weasel (smile), will once again experience the joy of being reunited under the starry canopy of heaven's glorious light.

Then, and only then, will we understand that the shadows of our nocturnal pain were but preparation of a day without end.

Yes, then, my darling daughter, all the disjointed fragments of our lives on earth will be joined together in the harmonious jubilance of angels singing and joy bells ringing; our lives stretched out before us in a breathtaking perpetual sunrise.

So until then, my first born, I will be walking toward the horizon of the new day that awaits our inseparable hearts in the not-too-distant future.

As for now, that which in days gone by was but nocturnal agony will one day burst forth in the splendor of a new day, in a new place, in a new time known as eternity.

A time when our hearts will race like the wind toward God's warm embrace, and the pain we once knew that had its genesis in Charlotte, many years ago, will have its fullest revelation on yonder's celestial shores.

THE MAKING OF A DEACONESS: YOUR STORY

Briefly write your own story.
_____
_____
_____
_____
_____
_____
_____

Describe your thorn in the flesh.
_____
_____
_____

How has God's grace been sufficient?
_____
_____
_____

What passages of Scripture have been particularly helpful to you?

_____

_____

_____

_____

_____

How could a deaconess have helped you?

_____

_____

_____

How will you help others as a result of your experience?

_____

_____

_____

Section II

THE MAKING OF A DEACONESS: BIBLICAL MINISTRY TO WOMEN

*Jesus would be in her a well of water
"springing up into everlasting life"*

John 4:14

WOMEN AROUND THE WELL

Read John 4:10-15

In John 4, we find a Samaritan woman who had come to what was known as Jacob's Well to draw water. She had come to the well at the sixth hour (noon), most likely to avoid her enemies and detractors. As a woman of Samaria, she was considered racially impure. She was a part of a group that was considered ethically contaminated. Samaritans were Jews whose blood was mingled with the blood of Gentiles. To have interaction or dealings with a Samaritan was to place oneself in need of ceremonial cleansing. Samaritans were shunned, ridiculed, and ostracized, much like women of color today.

Most upstanding citizens of Samaria would go to the well in the cool of the early morning or late evening. Only the undesirables, such as prostitutes, or weary travelers would go to the well at the hottest time of the day. When the Samaritan woman arrived that day, she had no idea she would discover Jesus, the well of "living water (v. 10)," the well from which, if she drank, she would never thirst again. Jesus would be in her a well of water "springing up into everlasting life" (v. 14).

The Samaritan woman was a victim of many broken marriages. In John 4, we find that she had five marriages that ended in divorce. Just think, she had been told by five husbands that she was no longer wanted. She had to endure the sting of being rejected five times. This lonely woman had to live with the fact that five men, after having been *with* her, decided they no longer *wanted* her. She had to endure five times of being made to feel she was not pretty enough, not shapely enough, just plain not *woman* enough to keep the attention of a man. It is not difficult to see why her self-esteem was so low, if not at rock bottom. It is not difficult to understand why she seemed to settle for a "shacking" arrangement. I have never talked with a woman who felt good about shacking, even with it's sophisticated title of "co-habitation." But when you live a life of rejection, as was the case with this woman, you get to the point where you reject your own self-worth. All too often, women come to the well of the church, where they are supposed to meet Jesus, but they meet rejection again. Instead of receiving living water, they are victimized by the pious, self-righteous judgment of scornful women of the church. Where else are they expected to go?

The Samaritan woman also seemed not to have a father to whom she could turn. The text is silent as to her family or father, but the need of a father in a woman's life is immeasurable. I want to impress upon men everywhere who have fathered girls how important they are to their daughters' lives. Yours was the first relationship she ever had with a member of the opposite sex. Yours was the first masculine hand she ever held, the first masculine voice she ever heard. You set the standard by which all other men are judged. Her relationship with you is vital if she is ever to see men as God desires for her to see them. So much of what you do and so much of what you say will affect her long after you will have gone on to be with the Lord. In fact, you will never die, as long as she lives. You will still be influencing her thinking, her way of relating to others, especially men, and her view of herself. Men of this day, your daughters need you. Go to them. Put your arms around them. You represent a safe haven from the wolves of this world. It's not too late. She is waiting for you.

Besides her father, the Samaritan woman had at least six men in her life who treated her less than a woman of value. Is there any wonder why she began to fend for herself? However, she still had a thirst. She needed to know that someone cared for a six-time loser. Churches are full of women like this Samaritan woman. Women who long to belong. Women who want to be free from the painful feelings of rejection. Women who need to feel good about themselves. This Samaritan woman wanted to be whole, so she said to the Master, "Give me this water" (v.15). I believe in making this request, she knew she was asking for something more than mere H_2O. She was asking for her freedom—freedom from shame, rejection, frustration, loneliness, and emptiness.

Jesus was the seventh man in the life of this Samaritan woman (five marriages and the man she resided with at the time of the text). Seven is the number of perfection, completion, and wholeness. Do not stop until you, too, have come to your place of completion and wholeness. You, too, will discover this can only occur when you have a personal encounter with Jesus by the well.

After the resurrection and ascension of Jesus, the church, the body of Christ on earth, became that well, and there are many women with problems, burdens, and scars at the well who are hoping to find living water to satisfy their great thirst for freedom and deliverance. The Samaritan woman had several areas in her life that needed to be impacted by the living water of the Savior, and many women today are also hurting in some of these same areas.

Women of color face racial discrimination and are often victimized by the bitter attitudes of those who consider themselves superior. African American women are often forced to tolerate prejudices associated with race, gender, and socioeconomics on a global and communal level, including in the workplace and the worship place. Even Black men participate in the discrimination of Black women. Women come to the well every Sunday morning asking for the water that Jesus spoke about, asking for the substance about which Solomon wrote in

Proverbs 25:25, "As cold water to a thirsty soul, so is good news from a far county (NKJV)." In the following sections, we will discuss a few of the other burdens that women may struggle with as they come to the well.

WOMEN AROUND THE WELL

As cold water to a thirsty soul, so is good news from a far country.
Proverbs 25:25, NKJV

Have you tasted of that water? Explain.

_____
_____
_____
_____

Have you drunk from that well out of which flows "living water?" Explain.

_____
_____
_____
_____

Can you identify with this woman in any way?

_____

Can you identify with her experience with racial prejudice?

_____

In what way have you suffered rejection like this woman of Samaria?

_____
_____
_____

Have men let you down in your life? If so, explain.

_____
_____
_____

Why do you think men have such an impact upon women?

_____
_____
_____

Do you feel like a victim? Why?

_____
_____
_____

Can you remember an encounter with Jesus at the well of your church?

Date

_____

Circumstance

_____

_____

_____

With whom have you shared your testimony?

_____

What passages of Scripture are particularly encouraging to you in your quest to become "whole"?

_____

_____

_____

THE WOMAN CAUGHT IN ADULTERY

Read John 8:1-11

One of the greatest destroyers of self-esteem is guilt. Women, in particular, are victimized by guilt because there is been a double standard in our society. In the minds of many, women are held to a higher standard in the areas of moral discrepancies than men. Ever since I was a little girl, I have been told that men can wallow in dirt, get up, dust themselves off, put on a suit, go to church, and receive respect. However, the women they wallowed with do not enjoy the same privileges. Oftentimes, the women must carry the stain, the scarlet letter 'A,' for the rest of their lives.

The woman in John 8 finds herself in such a dilemma. She is not only found in chapter 8 of our text, however; she is found in every segment of our society, from the White House to the church house. She may be wearing an evening gown, business suit, or Daisey Dukes, but inside, the scarlet letter burns her to shame. It seems that no level of education or volume of praise can eradicate the guilt she carries. Unbeknownst to the men in our text, they did the woman a great service. They brought her to Jesus. Their bringing was for the purpose of condemnation, but the ultimate result was liberation. Ought not deaconesses do likewise? Is it not one of the primary duties of the deaconess to take women riddled and burdened with guilt from condemnation to liberation?

WOMAN CAUGHT IN ADULTERY

1. In your opinion, are the motives of many in the church like those men who brought this woman to Jesus?

   _____
   _____
   _____
   _____

2. Is there a double standard in the church as relates to men and women? If so, explain.

   _____
   _____
   _____
   _____

3. How did Jesus address the double standard? (v. 6-7)

   _____
   _____
   _____
   _____

4. What do you think Jesus wrote on the ground?

   _____
   _____
   _____

5. What do you think were the results of Jesus' approach to this woman's sin?

   _____
   _____
   _____

6. How can deaconesses utilize such an approach?

   _____
   _____
   _____

7. In your opinion, what were this woman's feelings as she departed from Jesus?

   _____
   _____
   _____

8. How did you handle your guilt after you met Jesus?

   _____
   _____
   _____

ABIGAIL: THE WOMAN MARRIED TO NABAL

Read I Samuel 25:1-39

Abigail was a godly woman, but she was married to an alcoholic named Nabal. Like many alcoholics, Nabal provided for his family, but also, like many alcoholics, Nabal could be very foolish and offensive. Because of his foolish behavior, Nabal put his entire household at risk.

Nabal had a very short memory regarding the source of his blessings, so instead of being thankful to his benefactor (David), he treated him offensively. In doing so, Nabal exposed his household to the wrath, rather than the respect, of his lord. Nabal did not want to give back a portion of his blessings, so he faced the consequences of losing them all.

Many women find themselves in Abigail's shoes. Wives often suffer terrible consequences as a result of the ungodly actions or sinful behavior of their husbands. Their husbands fail to show respect or honor and do not give back to the source of their blessings. Many wives suffer in silence and rarely get an opportunity to even express an opinion.

Women can learn from Abigail, a godly woman who was determined that she was not going to allow her alcoholic, abusive, and offensive husband to take the blessings of her Lord away from her household.

The story of Abigail is all too common for many women of today: their past painful, their present miserable, and their future bleak, all because of husbands who believe they are bigger than God. Surely, women can learn from Abigail, a godly woman who was determined that she was not going to allow her alcoholic, abusive, and offensive husband to take the blessings of her Lord away from her household.

Application

ABIGAIL: THE WOMAN MARRIED TO NABAL

1. In what specific area did Nabal offend his Lord? v. 10-11

   _____
   _____
   _____

2. Upon hearing how her husband had offended her lord, what were the actions of Abigail? v. 18-31

   _____
   _____
   _____

3. What should be the actions of women today when their husbands offend our Lord?

   _____
   _____
   _____

4. What should be the financial actions of a woman whose husband offends God in such a way?

_____
_____
_____

5. What would you identify as the most outstanding quality of Abigail?

_____
_____
_____
_____

6. Are the actions of Abigail in verse 19 commendable?
Yes _____ No _____ (She told not her husband). Explain.

_____
_____
_____

7. What do you suppose Abigail's relationship with her husband was like?

_____
_____
_____

8. Is your relationship with your husband, in any way, like Abigail's relationship with Nabal? Explain.

_____
_____

9. Do you sometimes, within the secret chambers of your heart, fantasize a David coming along and rescuing you? (Don't write your answer!)

10. How often do you go to the Lord about your relationship with your husband?

    _____
    _____
    _____

11. Did Abigail have any forewarning as to the character of her husband before marriage? (Remember the name "Nabal" means "foolish")

    _____
    _____
    _____

12. Do you think that Abigail loved her husband? Explain your answer.

    _____
    _____
    _____

13. Was Abigail disrespectful to her husband when she called him a "man of Belial?" (Belial means "Satan.") Explain your answer.

    _____
    _____
    _____

RUTH AND NAOMI: WOMEN IN NEED OF FRIENDSHIP

One of the greatest and most rewarding assets a growing believer can possess is a godly friend. Genuine friendship is the most precious relationship of all. If a woman can, in an entire lifetime, develop just one true and lasting friendship, she can consider herself highly blessed. A real and godly friend can represent the sustaining hand of God through life's greatest trials and most turbulent storms. Genuine friendship is more valuable than worldly wealth, for it responds to one's every pain with presence and ministers to one's deepest need with compassion. Friendship, true friendship, endures distance, disappointment, and disaster with a loving word and a tender embrace.

> *One of the greatest and most rewarding assets a growing believer can possess is a godly friend.*

God's word encourages friendship:

"A friend loveth at all times"
Proverbs 17:17

"Faithful are the wounds of a friend"
Proverbs 27:6

"Thine own friend, and thy father's friend, forsake not"
Proverbs 27:9

Two of the greatest love stories the world has ever known are found in the pages of God's Word. One is the story of David and Jonathan. The other is that of Ruth and Naomi. What makes these two love stories unique is that they both involve friends. The Greek word for the love of a friend is *phileo*.

Ruth and Naomi were probably two of the most unlikely people to form a friendship because they were so opposite. One was young while the other was old. One had her life in front of her, the other behind. However, they were brought together at the intersection of grief and loneliness, and they decided to travel the road of life together, bound by friendship alone.

Read Ruth 1:1-18

Psalm 139 tells us that we are beautifully and wonderfully made. The name Ruth means beauty, and the name Naomi means *my pleasantness*. The friendship of an older woman who has gone through the storms of life without becoming bitter can bring out the beauty of a younger woman. Such was the case of Ruth and Naomi. Naomi had great tragedy and pain in her life. She lost her husband and her two sons, yet she did not become bitter nor did she try to inflict guilt upon her daughters-in-law. In verse 8, she blesses them with a benediction of compassion, "The Lord deal kindly with you." She offers similar words in verse 9, "The Lord grant you that ye may find rest, each of you in the house of her husband." Finally, she was affectionate toward them. She kissed them. Verse 10 illustrates that Ruth and Orpah were drawn to Naomi, as well. If young women today are going to be drawn to older women, to glean from their wisdom and experiences, then older women cannot possess a harsh, bitter spirit. Naomi treated both her daughters-in-law with love and respect, but Orpah chose to leave. Ruth, however, clung to her.

RUTH AND NAOMI: WOMEN IN NEED OF FRIENDSHIP

1. What was Naomi's desire for her two daughters-in-law? (v. 8-9)

   _____
   _____
   _____
   _____

2. Why did she desire such a blessing for her daughters-in-law? (v. 8)

   _____
   _____
   _____
   _____

3. What was the desire of Orpah and Ruth? (v. 10)

   _____
   _____
   _____

4. Why did Naomi attempt to send them away? (v. 12)

   _____
   _____

5. How would you describe the actions of Ruth verses the actions of Orpah? (v. 14)

   _____
   _____
   _____

6. In your opinion, which daughter-in-law possessed a character that did not focus on selfish need?

   _____
   _____

7. The friendship of Ruth and Naomi was based upon what priceless commodity?

   _____
   _____

8. Do you have a friendship that approaches the friendship of Ruth and Naomi?

   _____
   _____

9. What is the most rewarding aspect of that friendship? (Refer to question #8).

   _____
   _____
   _____

10. What was the crowning moment of that friendship? (Refer to question #8).

    _____
    _____
    _____

11. How has that friendship facilitated your spiritual growth? (Refer to question #8).

    _____
    _____
    _____

12. Can you truly say that your friendship is a gift from God?
    Yes_____ No_____ Explain.

    _____
    _____
    _____

13. How was that friendship cultivated?

    _____
    _____
    _____

14. How was that friendship nurtured?

    _____
    _____
    _____

15. How is that friendship being nurtured?

_____

_____

_____

16. How is that friendship celebrated?

_____

_____

_____

OTHER WOMEN AROUND THE WELL

There are many other women around the well of the church. These women carry awesome burdens. These women suffer the pain of life's debilitating wounds. They come to the well seeking solace, encouragement, and empowerment. They come to the well because they have discovered they have nowhere else to go. These women come asking the age-old triad of questions found in Jeremiah 8:22, "Is there no balm in Gilead; is there no physician there? Why then is not the health of the daughter of my people recovered?" These women must be met by caring and compassionate deaconesses speaking the affirming words of the African-American spiritual: *There is a balm in Gilead to make the wounded whole, there is a balm in Gilead to heal the sin sick soul.*[8]

Section III

MOVING FORWARD IN MINISTRY:
HOW A DEACONESS CAN MAKE A DIFFERENCE

Now I introduce and commend to you our sister Phoebe, a deaconess (servant) of the church at Cenchrea, that you may receive her in the Lord [with love and hospitality], as God's people ought to receive one another. And that you may help her in whatever matter she may require assistance from you, for she has been a *helper of many, including myself.
Romans 16:1-2, Amplified

*"succourer of many, helper of many"
American Standard Version

*"defender of many"
The Emphasized Bible (J.B. Rotherham)

*"protector of many"
An American Translation (Edgar J. Goodspeed)

*"staunch friend to me and to many others"
The Twentieth Century New Testament

HOW A DEACONESS CAN MAKE A DIFFERENCE

I have often wondered how a deaconess could have made a difference in my life. Coming from a home where going to church was the order of the day, I wonder how different my life might be today had the church that was so much a part of my upbringing had an active and anointed deaconess ministry. I wonder how much pain could have been avoided. How many tears would not have been shed? I wonder if I would have had to experience two unplanned and out-of-wedlock pregnancies looking for love in all the wrong places. I wonder if I would have felt better about myself in the wake of the abandonment of the father I loved so dearly. Would I have ever moved to Washington, DC, running frantically from the horrors of Charlotte, NC, and the shame of a checkered past?

I often wonder how my life would have been different were there at least one deaconess who could have seen my need, felt my pain, and ministered to my spirit. I know that my life would be different, but I wonder how different. I suppose the lack of a caring deaconess early on in my life is part of the reason why I am so determined that no young woman in the church of which I am a deaconess will have to one day sit as I did, look through tear-tired eyes, and wonder how a deaconess could have made a difference in her life.

> *I often wonder how my life would have been different were there at least one deaconess who could have seen my need, felt my pain, and ministered to my spirit.*

As it relates to the church and its responsibility, we as deaconesses must make a difference in the lives of the women God has entrusted to us by imparting the love, wisdom, and resources that God has given to us. I wonder sometimes why I had to endure some of the pain, rejection, and humiliation that I experienced, even at the hands of so-called women of God—often thinking that nobody loves me or that I'm an embarrassment to my family—never believing that I could get up from my bed of shame and walk in the sunlight of God's forgiveness and love. I was not a hard-hearted or rebellious child, just one who allowed the sound of the world to direct and victimize me. I am convinced that a deaconess could have made a difference, a big difference, just by spending time with me.

A deaconess could have made a difference by sharing with me the things that life had thrown her way and testifying how the Lord had brought her out. Oh, how I needed to know that the Lord could bring me out! A deaconess could have made a difference by teaching me the principles of a virtuous woman and letting me know that one day, my price could be "far above rubies" (Proverbs 31:10). When I felt like a failure, I needed a woman of God to tell me that in Christ, I could be "more than [a conqueror]" (Romans 8:37). When I was afraid, I needed to hear that "God has not given [me] a spirit of fear, but of power and of love and of a sound mind" (2 Timothy 1:7 NKJV). However, as sad as it is to say, when I looked to the church to help me out of the mess I was in, there was no one available. There was plenty of good-intentioned help on Sunday morning as I cried out at the altar, but late at night, when the darkness of an ominous future frightened me to death, I was alone and lonely. I would drink alcohol, thinking it could give me courage. I had anger that I did not know what to do with, so I became numb to my real feelings and the feelings of others.

I worked hard at having a quick tongue, trying to guard my heart from future hurts. I went from man to man seeking the love I desired from my father. I made one mistake after another. I was afraid to open up to anyone for fear of being hurt. Oh, how I needed the caring hug of a deaconess to let me know there was another way to deal with the pain and fear that haunted my life.

BUILDING WOMEN

I see a great need for building women, beginning in early adolescence, before puberty. One might ask, "How can deaconesses build women?" My reply is, "From the inside out by educating them from the Word of God, and by the implementation of ministries, workshops, and seminars designed to teach them to utilize the Word of God in a practical way in their lives."

Deaconesses can make a difference in the lives of young women simply by teaching them God's purpose in their lives. It is important, at an early age, to know that you are special and that God had a plan and purpose in mind when He made you. Pre-teens need to be taught to know God's plan and purpose for their lives so they can begin to realize who they are. As life begins to unfold, teens need to be taught to pursue their purpose and take a stand for what they know is right. Teens must know how to combat the fears of growing up. As their bodies begin to develop and things start happening socially, teens need to be educated by the church instead of being programmed by the world.

TEACHERS OF GOOD THINGS (8 TRAITS)

The aged women likewise, that they be in behavior as becometh holiness, not false accusers, not given to much wine, teachers of good things; that they may teach the young women to be sober, to love their husbands, to love their children, to be discreet, chaste, keepers at home, good, obedient to their own husbands, that the word of God be not blasphemed. (Titus 2:3-5)

Some might think that older women and younger women are not compatible. First duty of the deaconess in the church today is to get rid of the false notion that there is a natural enmity between older women and younger women. In our text, notice that Paul does not address any enmity or strife between older and younger women. In my opinion, the greatest asset that a young woman can have in today's society is a close relationship with an older, godly woman. The wisdom of an older woman who possesses Christian wisdom and godly virtue can serve as a powerful catalyst for a younger woman. Therefore, if younger women today are going to rise above those obstacles or hindrances that tend to keep them imprisoned in a valley of exploitation and despair, the notion of a natural enmity between older women and younger women must be dispelled.

> *Deaconesses can make a difference in the lives of young women simply by teaching them God's purpose in their lives.*

The responsibility to dispel this notion rests squarely on the shoulders of the older, Christian women. We must be comfortable and content with our present station in life so that we do not subconsciously harbor any envy toward our younger counterparts, who are in the spring of their lives. We must never seek to engage in the foolish act of competing with our daughters, nieces, and younger companions in Christ. God has called us to be companions and not competitors, allies and not adversaries, to this present-day generation of His young daughters. All too often, you see women in the fall of their lives trying to recapture the spring. As we age in Christ, our beauty should move inward and serve as an incubator that nurtures the young. The younger women of the church should not have to compete with deaconesses while they are in the process of confronting the devil. Before you give of your advice, you should give of your love to the young people today. They do not care how much you know until they know how much you care.

The greatest service a deaconess can perform on behalf of younger women is to impart unto them the qualities recommended in Titus 2:3-4. In the pastoral epistle of Titus, Paul instructs the *aged women*—those women whose behavior could be described as *becometh holiness*, who were not *false accusers, not given to much wine*—to be *teachers of good things*. Thus, he employs them to teach the young women the *eight traits of a godly woman*. These traits would teach younger women how to please God in their day-to-day walk with Christ. I am convinced beyond a shadow of a doubt that if deaconesses would be about teaching younger women, both by precept and by example, the eight qualities described in Titus 2:4 and 5, younger women would be spared the pain, distress, loneliness, degradation, and often, the self-inflicted abuse from which they suffer in this society. The *eight traits* are as follows.

First, "Be sober!" To *be sober* is to be wise, to keep one's head about oneself. To be a thinker and not one who allows emotion to eradicate common or spiritual sense. Sobriety does not only suggest that one should not be intoxicated with strong drink or illicit drugs, but young women can become intoxicated with romance or a need for affection. There is absolutely nothing more intoxicating to a young woman than a handsome young man saying all the things to her that she not only *desires* to hear but, in many cases, also desperately *needs* to hear. The wise deaconess will encourage young women to recognize the areas in which they are most vulnerable and therefore guard their hearts against the exploitation of these areas by those who seek to seduce them. First Peter 5:8 says, "Be sober, be vigilant; because your adversary the devil, as a roaring lion, walketh about, seeking whom he may devour."

I wish a thousand times that a deaconess, between my father's death and my relationship with the man for which I bore two children out of wedlock, would have taught me to be sober!

Second, Paul instructed the older women to teach the younger women "to love their husbands." I have found it difficult to teach younger women to *love their husbands* in this society because many young women are not certain what love is. Many young women today have never experienced real love. As a deaconess, I see many, many women who do have the foggiest notion what the word love means, how love feels, or what love does. They have never had anyone to truly love them for themselves.

They have experienced people, especially men, who have loved them because they have large breasts, nice legs, a cute smile, or a voluptuous figure. I feel that before deaconesses can teach younger women to love their husbands, deaconesses must teach them to *recognize* their husbands before the wedding ring goes on, and certainly before the first romantic interlude. The husband is charged to love her for who she is and not for what she can provide for him, and definitely not for how she can serve as an ornament or trophy for his ego.

In accordance to this admonition to teach younger women to love their husbands, the deaconesses in the local church should set about the task of teaching younger women, by precept and by example, through their own spousal relationships. Many of today's young women were not blessed to be brought up in the household with a father and a mother. Therefore, many younger women have never witnessed a woman loving her husband. Thus, the only way she can learn to love her husband is to be taught. It is the responsibility of the deaconesses to teach younger women what it is to love their husbands, yet maintain their own dignity and self-esteem.

Third, Paul admonishes deaconesses to teach younger women to "love their children." This is becoming increasingly important because today's young mothers often are forced to wear many hats. More and more women are serving as heads of households, and they must fulfill the responsibility of providing part, if not all, of the children's support. They must maintain a proper balance of child rearing, effective housekeeping, career development, and church membership. The multifaceted responsibilities are often overwhelming, especially in the demanding, exasperating area of child rearing. It often seems one's entire existence is controlled by the cry of "Mama!" The truth of the matter is that Mama needs help being Mama. Where can she find help other than from the experienced and wise deaconess? The deaconesses can provide the young mother with the vital assistance she desperately needs to love her children!

I often reflect upon my experience of having to love my children while at the same time attempting to provide for them and maintain a decent household. I can only thank God that I did not go completely out of my mind in the process. It would have been helpful to have someone to lean on in my moments of great frustration and exasperation. I needed the loving touch of a deaconess, if for no other reason than to encourage me in those lonely, frightening hours when I would lie awake searching for a reason to go on.

Fourth, deaconesses must teach younger women to "be discreet." To *be discreet* is to exhibit good judgment. Good judgment is a by-product of wisdom. Wisdom, true wisdom, comes from God. The deaconess is God's representative in fleshly form.

Every young woman needs a deaconess to assist her in areas that require discretion. Today's world is vastly different from yesterday's world. There are infinitely more choices to be made, many of which will determine her future mental and emotional stability. From the selection of household products to husbands, as well as other frightening choices, decisions can be difficult to make without the wise counsel that a deaconess can provide. The ministry of deaconess is not merely for a great, public ceremonial show; instead, it is one of being there when people, especially young women, are in need of godly advice.

Fifth, Paul charges the deaconess to teach younger women to "be chaste." The deaconess, above all others in the body of Christ, knows the importance of the sexual purity of young women. It is not enough for deaconesses to assist in serving communion on Sunday morning, deaconesses must be about the task of teaching young women the importance of maintaining their purity. Not only must deaconesses teach the *what* of sexual purity, but more importantly, they must teach the *why* and the *how* of sexual purity.

In a society that exploits the physicality of women, deaconesses must launch and maintain an offensive to protect young women from sexual exploitation and abuse. The ear of the deaconess ought to be attuned to the cries of those who have been victimized by this perverted, sexually-sick society. Who else but deaconesses are more fit to teach the younger women of the church? Male pastors can only go so far, only do so much, and maintain their positions as pastor. The failure of deaconesses in teaching younger women to be chaste puts pastors and male leaders of the church at risk. Deaconesses must shoulder the responsibility to teach younger women to *be chaste*.

Sixth, "be keepers at home." The phrase *keepers at home* has to do with the focus of young housewives in their own homes. In 1 Timothy 5:13 Paul, makes reference to the dangers of idleness and the misuse of leisure time among younger women. He warns how they, "learn to be idle, wandering about from house to house; and not only idle, but tattlers also and busybodies, speaking things which they ought not."

The divine duty of deaconesses is to teach women, especially younger, married women to focus on their own homes and to attend to their own affairs. It is easy for young women to fall victim to the lure of getting the inside scoop on what's going on in the homes of others, while neglecting their own. The world in which we live today has gone mad dabbling into the affairs of others. The popularity of supermarket tabloids, social media, and reality television stimulates the fascination of those who squander away their time following the latest gossip. In my church, one of the elderly deacons has popularized the slogan, "Six months I ought to mind my business, and the other six months I ought to leave other people's business alone." If the home and family are to be what God has designed them to be, deaconesses must be about the business of teaching younger women to be *keepers at home*. Younger women need to be taught the art of being housewives, which seems to be rapidly becoming obsolete in this generation.

With demands on her time in so many areas, the young housewife today has less time to spend in the home than the housewives of yesterday. Therefore, deaconesses in local churches should sponsor seminars and workshops on "Using Time Effectively" and "Cleaning, Cooking, and General Housekeeping." It is very easy to stand back and criticize young women, but the challenge of modern deaconesses is to roll up their sleeves and make a difference.

It is sad, but painfully true, that many young women today

are taught more by reality television and social media than by serious-minded deaconesses. Consequently, they are deceived and fall victim to "those who creep into households and make captives of gullible women loaded down with sins, led away by various lusts, always learning and never able to come to the knowledge of the truth" (2 Timothy 3:6-7 NKJV).

How sad, indeed.

Often, deaconesses spend too much time addressing the pettiness and shenanigans of the older, stiff-necked women of the congregation and miss the calling to *teach the younger women*! Some argue the reason why deaconesses avoid reaching out to and teaching younger women is the generation gap. I contend, however, that the task of reaching out to younger women often intimidates older women. It overwhelms them. It is too challenging. It is easier to dress in white uniforms, assist in baptism, serve communion, and look pious than to get in the trenches with young people and make a difference. However, it is time that deaconesses take off their white gloves and begin to take younger women by the hand and say, "I know we speak different languages, I know we're from different generations, I know there is a preconceived notion that we are somehow at odds with each other, but I'm here for you. I love you, and I'm willing to do whatever it takes to help you glorify God." That is how deaconesses can make a difference in the lives of the young women of this generation!

Seventh, Paul admonishes the aged women to teach the younger women *goodness*. Today, like never before, younger women need to be taught to "be good." Deaconesses must teach younger women the values of virtue. The question of "Who can find a virtuous woman?" is still being asked, especially in the western world. In this culture, it appears that more value is put on the sensuality of one's body than the spirituality of one's heart. It seems that almost as soon as little girls are able to walk, they are being entered into beauty pageants instead of the primary Sunday School class. Girls wear make-up, mini-skirts, nylon stockings, and high heels as young as six years old. It seems as if morality is not being taught in the church. Young women should learn from an early age the importance of developing a godly set of morals instead of their bust line. If deaconesses fail in this area, they fail—period.

As a deaconess in the local church, I am often driven to tears as I see the sad evidence of the failure of our predecessors in the area of teaching goodness. The tragic evidence of this failure is seen as I observe young women walking down the street with cigarettes hanging from their lips. I see this failure as I observe young women standing on street corners dressed like hookers and cursing like sailors. I see this failure when I observe young women who treat their bodies as legal tender, or a medium of exchange, to get the attention from young men that they should have received from their fathers. I see this failure as I counsel young women as young as 14 years old who have had more than one abortion, or as young as 16 who have more than one child.

When I look out among young women today, I see the horrible ruins of young women who have become casualties on this spiritual battlefield. I see young women who have had all the fight taken out of them and who have come to respond to the name of the "B" word. Believe it or not, many of these young women were brought up in the church. They are our daughters, granddaughters, nieces, and little sisters who have not so much as heard that there is another side to the deaconesses than to sit in front of the church dressed in white on Sunday morning and hardly speak after the benediction.

The deaconesses of today must begin to see that their duty extends far beyond the walls of the sanctuary of the local church. At some point, deaconesses must see that until their ministry reaches the hearts of young women, it has not gone far enough. Deaconesses must teach younger women the quality that makes their price far above rubies.

Finally, Paul admonishes the aged women to teach the younger women to "be obedient to their own husbands." As a deaconess, who from time to time is called upon to engage in premarital counseling, I have found that this is one of the most difficult responsibilities to convey to young women. It is difficult, in my opinion, because deep down within the heart of the prospective bride, she fears that the young man she is considering as a husband may not be a Christian. Therefore, I find that the *obey your husband* lesson is best taught before you *select* your husband. You ought to select a husband that you have no problem obeying because the prospective husband is in Christ. It is much easier and less complicated to obey a husband who is obedient to Christ. The deaconess must teach, however, that the admonition to obey one's husband is, in reality, an admonition to obey God, who gives the command. Therefore, if a request is made of the wife to do something that is against God's Word, the request is made void by the higher authority.

The deaconess must also teach that the admonition to obey your husband is aptly worded "obey *their own* husbands"—not everyone else's husband. It ought to be made plain that this command of God is not a command for women to be submissive to *all* men, as if to say women are inferior to men. Every believer is commanded to "obey them that have the rule over you" (Hebrews 13:17); thus, we are to do so because of the position and not the gender.

Finally, concerning obeying your own husband, deaconesses must define for younger women the word *obey*. The obedience referred to in this passage does not mean "worship," "never to question," or "never to offer one's opinion." According to Matthew Henry, in this context, obey means, "a loving subordination, to prevent disorder or confusion, and to further all the ends of the relationship,"—not a slavish subjection. Deaconesses, it is our duty to "rightly [divide] the word of truth" (2 Timothy 2:15).

MOVING FORWARD IN MINISTRY:
HOW A DEACONESS CAN MAKE A DIFFERENCE
BUILDING WOMEN • 8 TRAITS

1. As you look around your church, neighborhood, or even your workplace, what would you determine to be the greatest need of the young women?

    a) Love [ ]

    b) Encouragement [ ]

    c) Friendship [ ]

    d) Spiritual Guidance [ ]

    e) Teaching them how to carry themselves as young ladies (especially around men) [ ]

    f) Acceptance [ ]

2. Whom do you feel God has anointed and commissioned to help fulfill that need?

    _____

3. Complete the following: "The aged (spiritually mature) women likewise, that they be in behavior as becometh (Titus 2:3)

    _____

4. What has God gifted you to teach young women as it relates to:

   a. being sober _____
   b. loving their husbands _____
   c. loving their children _____
   d. being discreet _____
   e. being chaste _____
   f. being keepers at home _____
   g. goodness _____
   h. being obedient to their own husbands _____

5. Do you think that verse 6 of this epistle to Titus is addressed to deaconesses in any way? Explain your response.

   _____
   _____

6. Can spiritually mature women teach young men to:

   a. be sober minded [ ] Yes [ ] No
   b. show a pattern of good works [ ] Yes [ ] No
   c. demonstrate incorrupt doctrine [ ] Yes [ ] No
   d. be sincere [ ] Yes [ ] No
   e. practice sound speech [ ] Yes [ ] No

7. What, specifically, are you doing in any of these areas?

   _____
   _____

The aged women likewise, that they be in behaviour as becometh holiness, not false accusers, not given to much wine, teachers of good things. (Titus 2:3)

Do you believe that the first step in developing "virtuous women" is that deaconesses must themselves be "virtuous"?
[ ] Yes [ ] No

8. According to Titus 2:3, in what four areas must deaconesses be virtuous?

   a) _____
   b) _____
   c) _____
   d) _____

9. In what areas should deaconesses focus in developing virtuous women? (v.4)

   a) _____
   b) _____
   c) _____

10. What qualities should be developed en route to be becoming virtuous? (v.5)

    a) _____
    b) _____
    c) _____
    d) _____
    e) _____

12. Are virtuous women born or developed? (Isaiah 53:6; Romans 3:23, 3:10; II Corinthians 6:17-18)

   _____
   _____
   _____
   _____
   _____

13. What is the first step in becoming a woman of virtue? (John 3:3; 2 Corinthians 5:17; Luke 6:39; Ephesians 4:11)

   _____
   _____
   _____

14. What is the first step in developing virtuous women?

   _____
   _____
   _____

15. In light of Matthew 15:14b, do you agree that the first step in developing virtuous women is that deaconesses must themselves be virtuous? Explain.

   > *"If one blind person guides another, they will both fall into a ditch."*
   >
   > Matthew 15:14b, NLT

   _____
   _____

16. What one word would you use to describe the state of women today?

   _____

17. Would you say that the stress of being a woman in today's society is overwhelming? [ ] Yes [ ] No   Explain.

   _____
   _____
   _____

18. Where can women go for help?

   _____
   _____

19. Is there any meaningful help for hurting women in your church, other than your pastor's Sunday morning sermon?

   _____
   _____

20. What kind of help does your church provide at this time?

   _____
   _____

SELF-ESTEEM

And in that day seven women shall take hold of one man, saying, 'We will eat our own food and wear our own apparel; only let us be called by your name, to take away our reproach.'
(Isaiah 4:1 NKJV)

In the verse above, we find Isaiah prophesying that a time will come when women will be in such dire need that seven of them will take hold of one man and say, "We are able to provide for ourselves (eat our own food and wear our own apparel), if you would only let us be called by your name to take away our reproach." I believe with all my heart that Isaiah was speaking about women of today. The women described in Isaiah 4:1 are reaching out in a desperate attempt to have their innermost need fulfilled by men: the need for a feeling of personhood, a sense of belonging, an identity (name). These women, however, are reaching out to get from men what they can only receive from God.

I have discovered that before we can reach a place of fulfillment in life, we must figure out *whose* we are because *who* we are is based upon *whose* we are. In working with women, single and married alike, I have witnessed the sad spectacle of women seeking to get their innermost need fulfilled by men. More and more women are becoming educated and able to provide for their own material need, but education alone leaves a vacuum that begs to be filled. That vacuum (that feeling of emptiness), however, can NEVER be adequately filled by

> *Only God can give us our true identity. Without a relationship with God, we will not have a healthy view of ourselves.*

a person in the human realm. That vacuum can only be satisfactorily filled by a relationship with God. Only God can give us self-worth. Only God can give us our true identity. Without a relationship with God, we will not have a healthy view of ourselves. God is the mirror into which we must gaze to see ourselves. Without God's mirror, we will constantly seek our identity by relating with others. Without God's mirror, we will have not only *low* self-esteem, but we will have *no* self-esteem.

Perhaps the best treatise I have read that deals with the self-esteem of women is that of Jack W. Hayford in his book *Divine Healing by the Power of the Holy Spirit*[9]. In the section "Healing and the Prayer of Faith," he examines the woman in Luke 8 who suffered for 12 years with an issue of blood. In a powerful exposition, he analyzes the woman's spiritually-impoverished condition and characterizes her transition to healing as "the touch of becoming." Wisely, Hayford does not address her financial poverty that resulted from 12 years of seeking a physical cure from earthly physicians. Instead, he addresses her poverty of spirit and argues that by finally reaching out and touching the Master, she became whole.

As women, we have needs that money cannot meet. Money can purchase medical insurance, but cannot purchase health. Money can purchase a membership into a social club, but cannot purchase friendship. Money can purchase a beautiful house, but it cannot purchase shelter from the storms of life. Money can purchase a college education, but it cannot purchase wisdom.

I have experienced the fruitless attempt to cure my spiritual aliments through financial means, but I discovered that a new dress or a new make-up line cannot bring about real beauty, fulfillment, or peace of mind. The realization for me was that money could not make me whole. A few years ago, I found myself earning more money than I ever dreamed I would when I stepped off the train in 1964; yet, I was more miserable than I had ever been in my entire life. What I needed, I could not get from a salary increase from my boss. What I needed, I could only receive by reaching out and touching the Master.

SELF-ESTEEM

1. Would you say that Isaiah 4:1 is descriptive of our day? Explain. [ ] Yes or [ ] No
   _____
   _____

2. What problems concerning women can you identify with that are prevalent today?
   _____
   _____

3. Is self-esteem a problem of Christian women today?
   _____

4. How can the church minister in the area of self-esteem to single, widowed, or divorced women today?
   _____
   _____

5. Has your pain, condition, or poverty of spirit made you feel like a nobody? Explain. [ ] Yes [ ] No
   _____

_____

_____

_____

6. Have you ever tried to purchase wholeness through financial means? Explain.

_____

_____

_____

7. What were the results? Discuss all that apply.

   a) Frustration?

   _____

   _____

   b) Indebtedness?

   _____

   _____

   c) Alienation?

   _____

   _____

   d) Other?

   _____

   _____

8. Prior to Jesus, to whom did you reach out for wholeness?

_____

_____

What were the circumstances?

_____

_____

What were the results?

_____

_____

9. Can you ever remember reaching out in an attempt to make contact with Jesus? Explain. [ ] Yes [ ] No

_____

_____

10. Read Luke 8:48. Have you developed a real and fulfilling relationship with the Lord? Explain. [ ] Yes [ ] No

_____

_____

11. Jesus encouraged the woman to "be of good comfort." Are you beginning to experience the comforting presence of Jesus in your life? Explain. [ ] Yes [ ] No

_____

_____

_____

12. What acts of faith are serving to make you whole?

_____

_____

13. Are you experiencing the peace of Jesus permeating within your person? Explain.

    _____
    _____

    In your home? Explain.

    _____
    _____

    In your vocation? Explain.

    _____
    _____

    In your church/ministry? Explain.

    _____
    _____

    In your children? Explain.

    _____
    _____

    In your friendships? Explain.

    _____
    _____

POWER BEGINS WITH "P"

Prayer

Never underestimate the power of prayer. The English writer Alfred Lord Tennyson said, "More things are wrought by prayer than the world has dreams of[10]." Godly homes and effective churches are not held together by bricks and mortar, by finances, or business expertise—but by prayer.

Prayer has wrought so much in my life. Prayer brought me from struggling as a frightened, unwed mother of two daughters in Charlotte, North Carolina to becoming the author of this book. Certainly, the wings of prayer have carried me this far.

Prayer was my only ally against the awful drudgery of my daughter's drug addiction. Like the woman in Luke 18, I travailed through my daughter's affliction for 18 years. Prayer kept my sanity and kept my child from any great harm. Prayer was also the single strand that held my world together when it seemed to unravel against the tidal wave of inner-city ghetto living, and it was prayer that connected my shaking hand reaching out in the darkness of misery to the steady, sure hand of Almighty God. When all others said there was no hope, through prayer, I heard the soft but assuring voice of God saying, "I will deliver thee and thy child." Women, pray without ceasing.

In Acts 12, when Peter was in prison in chains, the church of God prayed without ceasing, and evidence seems to suggest that those prayers came from the women of the church.

POWER BEGINS WITH "P": PRAYER

1. In Acts 12, what were the results of prayer?

2. Where did Peter go after he was delivered? (Acts 12:12)

3. Who answered the door?

4. What was the response to the women's prayer? (Acts 12:15-16)

5. Can you remember a time when your answered prayer was so immediate and powerful that you were amazed? Explain.

Patience

Perhaps the greatest obstacle between the Egypt of your despair and your Promised Land of deliverance is the dry, barren Sinai desert called Time. Time can be the most exasperating enemy of them all. Time can take faith and twist it into a sobbing, shaking, sniffling mess.

In 1964, I left my Egypt of Charlotte, NC en route to my Promised Land of Washington, DC. My journey to Washington, DC lasted a little more than nine hours. My journey to deliverance, however, lasted sixteen years. The oasis of my healing came into view 12 years ago. My journey has been arduous, soul wrenching, and sporadic, to say the least, but when your oasis of healing comes into view—God's divine love and providence becomes a beautiful reality.

When I look back across the years of my journey, I see God's divine hand brightening even my darkest hours, my most painful and lonely moments, and even my episodes of faithlessness to His glory. Therefore, I can say to women in pain everywhere, be encouraged because Time is no match for an omnipotent, omnipresent, omniscient God.

Several biblical examples prove that time withers when it stands before the Almighty God. In Matthew 9:20, we find a woman who suffered with an issue of blood for _____ years. In Luke 13, we find a woman who suffered with an infirmity for_____ years. In John 5:5, we find a man lying at the pool of Bethesda with an infirmity for_____ years. In John 9:1, we find a man who had been blind from _____. Each one of these individuals, like many of us, had to struggle against the awesome foe called Time. However, each found that Time was no match, nor their infirmity a strong opponent, against the Master. You must believe that Jesus was called Master because He is Master.

POWER BEGINS WITH "P": PATIENCE

Let's focus on that nameless woman we find in Luke 13:11.

1. Where did Jesus encounter this woman? (v. 10)

2. What does Luke say in terms of her ability to help herself? (v. 11)

3. What was the woman's real problem? (v. 16)

4. What were Jesus' seven words of deliverance? (v.12)

5. In your opinion, did Jesus lay hands on her?

   _____

   _____

6. What was her immediate response? (v. 13)

   _____

   _____

7. What were the reactions of the rulers of the synagogue? (v. 14)

   _____

   _____

8. How did Jesus compare the traditional response of religious leaders toward the cattle versus toward this woman? (v. 15)

   _____

   _____

9. What then should be our response to tradition? (v.17)

   _____

   _____

10. How did the people of that day respond to Jesus' casting aside tradition?

    _____

    _____

11. In what ways is the church of today like the synagogue of Jesus' day in terms of tradition?

   _____

   _____

12. In what ways are you like this woman?

   _____

   _____

Persistence

Having addressed the oftentimes menacing obstacle of time, as relates to our healing and deliverance, let us now focus on another discouraging barrier, the opinion and limitation of man. When I was growing up, people often told me I would not amount to anything. I was told I was too light complexioned and too skinny, with feet that were too big. They said these challenges would destroy my chances for any kind of joy and happiness in life. These statements robbed me of my self-esteem and left me in the wilderness of hopelessness. However, Romans 3:4 reached out to me and said, "Certainly not! Indeed, let God be true but every man a liar. As it is written: 'That you may be justified in your words, and may overcome when you are judged'" (NKJV).

I was also comforted by the words of Romans 1:17, "the just shall live by faith," and today, I am so glad I did not take the words of men and women—regardless how well intended, educated, or even spiritual they seemed to be—in regards to my worth with God. I believe that we as women ought to be persistent in our efforts and determination to be free, whole, and healed.

As women, we must be persistent in a world that consistently says "no" to women. We must be press forward in a world that constantly shuts doors in our faces and devalues our work and worth. We must demonstrate a godly resolve in our persistence. Our persistence must be fueled by faith, and our faith must be based upon God's Word. Faith and God's Word are our unseen advantage in a world that seeks to rob us of our hope. I say to women everywhere, persevere!

The many nameless women in the Bible are a great example of persistence. I am so glad the Word uses so many nameless women in relation to healing and wholeness because it lets us know that these women could be any one of us. I have developed the habit of putting my name in every instance in the New Testament where Scripture identifies a suffering woman. Doing this makes God's Word more personal.

POWER BEGINS WITH "P": PERSISTENCE

(Reference Mark 5:24-34 and Luke 8:43-48)

1. The nameless woman had been suffering with an issue of blood (hemorrhaging) for _____ years.

2. Luke 8:43 tells us that she had spent _____ her living upon to no avail. Thus, she went from sickness to poverty.

3. How does Mark 5:27 suggest she got to the place where Jesus was?

   _____
   _____

4. What would you say about her persistence?

   _____
   _____
   _____
   _____

5. How does your persistence compare to her persistence?

   _____
   _____

6. What was Jesus' response to the woman?
   _____
   _____

7. What did Jesus say as to what made her whole? (Mark 5:34)
   _____
   _____

Section IV

PREREQUISITES FOR DEACONESSES IN THE LOCAL CHURCH

The Spirit of the Lord is upon Me, because He has anointed Me to preach the gospel to the poor; He has sent Me to heal the brokenhearted, to proclaim liberty to the captives and recovery of sight to the blind, to set at liberty those who are oppressed.

Luke 4:18, NKJV

SELECTING DEACONESSES

Perhaps the most difficult responsibility a pastor or church can undertake is the divine task of selecting deaconesses. It takes more than regeneration, a positive attitude, Bible knowledge, or eloquence of speech to be a good deaconess. To be a good deaconess, a woman must possess a special burden to serve God and fallen humanity in general, and fallen womankind, in particular. To be a good deaconess takes an anointing like that found in Luke 4:18 (NKJV):

> The Spirit of the Lord is upon Me, because He has anointed Me to preach the gospel to the poor; He has sent Me to heal the brokenhearted, to proclaim liberty to the captives and recovery of sight to the blind, to set at liberty those who are oppressed.

I admonish pastors and churches to pray and pray and pray again before a woman is consecrated to the awesome office of deaconess. In this chapter, I attempt to set forth just a few of the prerequisites for deaconess in the local church. These prerequisites are by no means exhaustive, for I have learned there are no guarantees when it comes to selecting deaconesses. Through painful experience, I have learned that even with all the prerequisites and training, you can never be absolutely sure the woman you are laying your hands upon and consecrating into the office of deaconess will carry out the

> *The position of deaconess is not merely a title of honor that is bestowed upon older women in the church in recognition of many years of faithful service.*

office in a manner that will give glory to God and that is prescribed by the church.

As church leaders, all we can do is insure that we have set forth solid criteria and have developed a quality training program to equip the candidate with the necessary tools to do the job well. Even at that point, we will still find ourselves lying awake in the midnight hour, wondering if we made the right selection. The answer to that gut-wrenching question lies within the heart of the woman selected, the proof of which will be in her service and dedication to God. Therefore, in setting forth the following prerequisites, I put to you the question that Solomon rhetorically put forth over 3,000 years ago, "Who can find a virtuous woman (Proverbs 31:10)?"

INNER BEAUTY

The first quality that I feel is an absolute must for those who are being considered candidates for the office of deaconess in the local church is that of *inner beauty*. When I say inner beauty, I mean that certain spiritual attractiveness that seems to radiate from the innermost part of one's being. Inner beauty is a beauty of character, and not just of reputation. Inner beauty is a beauty that reflects a loyalty to the Savior, even when it costs popularity.

Inner beauty places integrity above cronyism and reconciliation above confrontation. In my estimation, inner beauty is just as apparent as external attractiveness and many times as important. Inner beauty understands what it is like to need a friend, a hug, or just an ear to listen. Inner beauty is that intangible quality that cannot be measured by one's knowledge of the Bible or memorization of various passages of Scripture. I am often reminded that the prophet Isaiah described the coming Messiah as having "no form nor comeliness" (53:2). Isaiah went on to say "and when we shall see Him, there is no beauty that we should desire Him (53:2)." However, we know that Jesus possessed an inner beauty that compelled Him to "preach the gospel to the poor," to "heal the brokenhearted," to "proclaim liberty to the captives and recovery of sight to the blind," and to "set at liberty them that are bruised (Luke 4:18 NKJV)."

If deaconesses are to be effective, their inner beauty must shine in this dark, wicked world as a beacon of hope to all those who inquire, "Is there a balm in Gilead?" (Jeremiah 8:22). To this desperate inquiry, inner beauty responds with gentleness and compassion so that the work of God might be done through her to make the wounded whole and to heal the sin-sick soul.

Inner beauty is the product of the Holy Spirit working in the hearts of those who avail and commit themselves to the ministry of hurting people. The Holy Spirit overshadows the heart of the willing believer and creates within that believer the gentle and quiet spirit that is necessary to be an effective deaconess. First Peter speaks of women whose "outward adorning" is not that of "plaiting the hair, and of wearing of gold, or of putting on of apparel" (3:3). This epistle goes on to employ women to "let it [their adorning] be the hidden man of the heart, in that which is not corruptible, even the ornament of a *meek* and *quiet* spirit, which is in the sight of God of great price" (emphasis added, 3:4). As the media exploits the outer appearance of women to sell almost anything from candy to cars, it reflects the world's standard of beauty. In the aforementioned verses, we are encouraged to adorn the "hidden man [person] of the heart." Thus, our emphasis ought to be that of adorning the spirit rather than the body.

It is important that deaconesses have the inner beauty of a gentle and quiet spirit. People are naturally attracted to a gentle- and quiet-spirited person. Gentleness is one of the manifestations of the fruit of the Holy Spirit (Galatians 5:22). Paul encourages all Christians to exemplify this character. The more we mature in Christ, the more we should seek to exemplify Him. We can start by working on our inner beauty, our quiet and gentle spirit—our inner person.

As life for the believer matures and blooms, it should be as a beautiful rose: The more the inner beauty is exposed, the better the fragrance. Our past lives may show off scars from the thorns on the stem, for thorns are unavoidable. Thorns make us uncomfortable, but I believe that we can work our way up through past hurts and pains and not permeate odious bitterness and anger. Instead, we can blossom with the sweet fragrance of a rose. What we nurture will grow, and what we neglect will die. We must nurture the inner person with the message from God that our beauty comes not from the outward adornment, but instead from the inner beauty of our gentle and quiet spirit.

The Character of a Deaconess

As president of the Deaconess Ministry of The Word of God Baptist Church, I am charged with training women who possess the inner beauty described above to serve in the awesome and challenging office of deaconess.

After discerning women who have inner beauty, I emphasize that deaconess candidates also must be fit in the following traits:

1) **Personal Fellowship**

    The deaconess should include in her daily schedule a period of private devotion. This period should consist of scriptural reading, mediation, and prayer. We are more fit for group and collective fellowship when we have fellowshipped personally with

God. When God communes with us, we can communicate His love to the crowd. Personal fellowship spawns commitment and steadfast devotion to God and kingdom causes.

2) **Stewardship**

   a. *Time* (Exodus 20:8-11; Revelation 4:11; Mark 1:35; Matthew 6:21)

   I have always felt the commandment to "Remember the Sabbath, to keep it holy" (Exodus 20:8) is a clear admonition to commit to the Lord at least one-seventh of our time (a day being one-seventh of a week). However, as I study Scripture, I am convinced that to even measure out or designate a portion of time to God is to be selfish and narrow-minded because we should always be seeking to give glory to God. Revelation 4:11 notes that we were created for God's pleasure. Therefore, whether we are chatting on the telephone or in the act of serving communion, we should be in the mode of bringing pleasure to God.

   We should also designate some specific time to God (Exodus 20:8). David reminds us to meditate in God's Word day and night (Psalm 1:2), so from the rising of the sun, as did Jesus (Mark 1:35), to the going down of the same, we should set aside time specifically for God. These times of devotion to God allow us to give glory to God in every area of our lives. Time is our most precious commodity. It would be almost materialistic of God to request a tenth of our resources and not more of our time. I have heard it said that love is spelled T-I-M-E. Jesus said in Matthew 6:21 that "where your treasure is, there your heart will be also" (NKJV). What greater treasure do we have on earth than our time? For a deaconess to be willing to tithe her income and not exceed the tithe in time is to reduce our God to a materialistic deity. No, my sisters, our God is much more than that. He is a God who is the eternal lover of our souls and longs to commune with us on a daily and continual basis.

b. *Tithe* (Malachi 3:8-12)

Some have erroneously claimed that tithing was under the dispensation of law, and since we live in the dispensation of grace, this nullifies any obligation on the part of believers to tithe. It will do them well to understand that tithing pre-dates the law, for we find in Genesis 14 that Abraham was a tither. Jesus says of tithing in Matthew 23:23, "These you ought to have done, without leaving the others undone" (NKJV).

c. *Talents* (Matthew 25: 14-30)

A talent, in regards to our responsibility to Christ, is anything He has given us to be used for the benefit of His Kingdom and to His glory. Talents vary, so each of us must first determine what our talents are and be careful to use them in a manner that pleases our Master. It should be the goal of all Christians to use all their possessions to the glory of our Lord and make all we have available to Him. It is not ours to determine what our talents are, but it is certainly our sacred duty to determine their use.

As seen in the parable of the talents, Our Lord has a way of increasing the talents of those who find a way to utilize and to multiply their talents as wise stewards. The automobile made available for the Master's use has a way of being upgraded by the Master. The one-bedroom apartment utilized for the Master's use has a way of being upgraded to a single-family home. The marginal singing voice used to praise the Maker of all has a way of developing into a magnificent instrument of praise. What talents have been entrusted to you? How are you using them? Are you using them in a way that will allow you to hear His voice say, "Well done, good and faithful servant; you have been faithful over a few things, I will make you ruler over many" (Matthew 25:23 NKJV)?

3) **Self-Denial**
    a. A deaconess must deny herself so that the cause of Christ might not be denied its place and its power
    b. A deaconess must deny herself so that the cause of Christ is not hindered

4) **Prioritizing Christ**
    a. A deaconess must put Christ before things (Matthew 6:33)
    b. A deaconess must put Christ before others (Matthew 10:37)
    c. A deaconess must put Christ before self (John 3:30)

5) **Conversation**
    a. A deaconess must not allow herself to be corrupted by corrupt communication. She must not give her mouth and her ears to gossip. Gossip can be defined in several ways: Gossip is talk about things not known to be true or factual. Gossip is talk about business that is not your own for no productive purpose. Gossip is the exercise of fools (see Ecclesiastes 5:3).
    b. I have learned from the study of Titus that a deaconess should in all things show herself as having a "pattern of good works; in doctrine showing integrity, reverence, incorruptibility, sound speech that cannot be condemned" (Titus 2:7-8 NKJV). Deaconesses must not be listed among those whom Paul speaks of as being "unruly and vain talkers and deceivers ... whose mouths must be stopped, who subvert whole houses, teaching things which they ought not (Titus 1:10, 11). A deaconess who makes a wise use of information and knowledge will be a woman of wisdom.

6) **Wisdom**

    The deaconess must be a companion to the pastor and deacons in wisdom. Deaconesses are:

    a. Admonished to be wise (Matthew 10: 16)
    b. A source of wisdom (Proverbs 1:7, James 1:5)

    c. Required to be a good listener (James 1:19)
    d. Expected to know the power and wisdom of real prayer (Acts 12:5)

7) **Faithful and "Faith-full"**

The Scripture tells us that without faith it is impossible to please God. As deaconesses, we simply will not be effective for the kingdom of God without faith. We must possess an undying, unshakable faith that God can and will do exactly what His Word says. Without faith, we are worthless to the kingdom and the churches in which we seek to serve. In Mark, we find that even Jesus could not do any "mighty work" in His hometown because of unbelief, "except that He laid His hands on a few sick people and healed them" (Mark 6:4-6 NKJV). If we deaconesses do not possess the simple faith necessary to do mighty works in our hometown, the church that bestowed upon us the title of deaconess, then we will be deaconesses in name only. We need to understand that faith is so key to this movement of Christianity that it is not called a *religion*, but rather a *faith*. Therefore, its adherents are called believers. Deaconesses must be chief among believers, for we must minister to women and men who, in many cases, simply have stopped believing.

When people respond to the invitation of discipleship, they do so with a measure of belief, but as life unfolds, sometimes their faith foundation begins to crumble. We must go forth and restore their faith. In reality, their faith will be increased in the same manner as ours, "Faith cometh by hearing, and hearing by the word of God" (Romans 10:17). However, the rhetorical questions that precede this declaration are "How shall they hear without a preacher? And how shall they preach, except they be sent?" (Romans 10:14b-15a). In many cases, the only preacher those who have lost their faith will ever hear may be the deaconess. Therefore, you must speak a word from the Lord to increase their faith. The deaconess must be *faith-full*!

The Scripture also instructs us to be faithful. There is nothing more discouraging to a pastor or church than a deaconess who is not faithful to the church or to the task assigned to her.

As president of the deaconess ministry of my church, I am personally appalled at the women who get glowing evaluations on their secular job for the quality of work rendered or for their faithfulness to the company, yet when they are called upon to do a work for the Lord, they can be described as slothful, at best. I am appalled at women who, before they were consecrated into the office of deaconess, were so faithful to the church, but after their consecration, they cannot be counted on to be at the weekly prayer service or monthly deaconess meeting. I get the feeling that after a while, they forget they are not so much accountable to the church or pastor, or even the president of the deaconess ministry, as they are accountable to God. The deaconess who is not faithful to the ministry of deaconess must not be tolerated, for she is a liability and not an asset to the deaconess ministry.

Deaconesses, the world over must be reminded that they are working toward the day when they hear the voice of our Lord say, "Well done, thou good and *faithful* servant" (emphasis mine, Matthew 25:21).

8) **Prayerful**

I would not give you two cents for a deaconess who does not pray. The deaconess who does not pray is dead weight in the deaconess ministry. Deaconesses must first understand that theirs is a spiritual—not ceremonial—ministry. Often, we have women who desire to be a deaconess because of the status of the position and not because of the call of the ministry. Churches around this world are suffering because they are filled with women who engage in the ministry of deaconess for social, rather than spiritual, reasons.

It is imperative that women selected for the ministry of deaconess are *women of prayer*. When I say women of prayer, I am not referring to women who pray very eloquent and charismatic public prayers, as did the Pharisees. When I use the phrase women of prayer, I mean women who have prayer as a priority in their private lives. A deaconess must remember that her strength, her direction, and her authority come from the Lord. A deaconess must be careful not to do anything of her own understanding but in all her ways acknowledge God, and He will direct her paths (Proverbs 3:6).

Deaconesses ought to gather regularly to pray for the concerns of the church. They ought to be constantly in a mode of prayer on behalf of the pastor, the deacons, and the church at large. There is absolutely no duty more important to the deaconesses than keeping the church lifted in prayer. The effective deaconesses are those who regularly beseech God to reveal those areas and persons in the church that are in greatest need of ministry. It is not enough for deaconesses to pray generally concerning the church. Conscientious deaconesses petition God to reveal those specific concerns that command prayer attention.

One of the watchwords of the deaconess ought to be *pre-prayered*. Deaconesses ought to engage in *pre-prayer*, prayer that concerns those things that have not yet proven to vex the church, but rather loom on the horizon. The pre-praying deaconess is often given insight into those things that are potential problems. Therefore, she sends up prayer in anticipation of such problems. I believe that many storms have been averted because the church has deaconesses who engage in the ministry of pre-praying.

9) **Spirit-Filled**

If the most important duty of the deaconess is that of prayer, and I certainly believe it is, then the most important attribute of a deaconess is to be Spirit-filled. We live in times that are filled with spirits, and not of the holy variety. John tells us, "Beloved, do not believe every spirit, but test the spirits, whether they are of God" (1 John 4:1 NKJV). The deaconess traffics in areas that require her to be filled with the Holy Spirit. It is not enough for a deaconess to be saved. It is not enough for a deaconess to have a general knowledge of God's Word. If deaconesses are to be effective companions in ministry with the pastor and deacons, deaconesses must be filled with the Holy Spirit.

Paul admonishes all believers in Ephesians 5:18, "And do not be drunk with wine, in which is dissipation; but be filled with the Spirit" (NKJV). Here, Paul is admonishing believers that we must be controlled by the Holy Spirit. When you are drunk with wine, you are controlled by alcohol, which is appropriately called a distilled spirit. Others can see the effect of distilled spirits in the walk and speech of someone under the influence because one does not have self-control, but is controlled by spirits outside of one's self.

The same applies for someone who is filled with the Holy Spirit. Just as the influence of alcohol is apparent in one who has imbibed in distilled spirits, the influence of the Holy Spirit is equally apparent. When one is filled with the Holy Spirit, one's walk and speech are different. When one is filled with the Holy Spirit, God's Word goes forth with awesome results, and the people of God will be wonderfully blessed. Deaconesses must constantly seek to be filled with God's Spirit. Personally, I cannot fathom one going forth to minister without the assurance of the Holy Spirit because what we seek to do under the banner of Christ is "'Not by might nor by power, but by My Spirit,' says the Lord of hosts" (Zechariah 4:6 NKJV).

10) **Outer Adornment**

   In like manner also, that the women adorn themselves in modest apparel, with propriety and moderation, not with braided hair or gold or pearls or costly clothing. (1 Timothy 2:9 NKJV)

It is the duty of the deaconess to set and enforce a dress code as outlined in 1 Timothy 2:9. To do so effectively, deaconesses must themselves avoid ostentatious or ornate styles of dressing. Godly women must adhere to the Biblical admonition of coming out from among the world, in terms of dress. Also, much care should be given to avoid arousing the carnal nature of men. Scripture clearly demonstrates that many godly men, from Samson to David, have been led down the road of lust, fornication, and adultery by visual stimulation from a woman, often unintentionally.

David might have avoided the sin that wreaked havoc in his household and caused God to forbid him from building the temple had he not seen the erotic sight of Bathsheba bathing on the rooftop. The very first words the mighty Samson quoted in Scripture were, "I saw a woman," and it was a woman that led to that damning haircut that sapped his God-given power. Job declared, "I have made a covenant with my eyes; why then should I look upon a young woman?" (Job 31:1 NKJV).

Inappropriately dressed women have led to the fall of some of God's mightiest of men. One of the purposes of the deaconess in the local church is to protect God's men in the areas they are most vulnerable, one of which is visual stimulation. Therefore, deaconesses ought to set the standard by example. The deaconess is also required, by precept, to impart the wisdom of modest apparel to the women of the church. When necessary, the deaconess should step forth in her God-given authority to see that the set standard is adhered to by all women of the church. Matthew 18:15-20 models how this standard should be enforced in the household of faith.

In a time that seems void of any godly standard, the deaconess must be the standard bearer in the local church concerning dress. No woman who does not already exemplify this standard should even be considered for consecration to the ministry. Any deaconess presently serving who does not comply to such a standard should be 1) advised, 2) reprimanded, and 3) removed, if necessary. First Timothy 2:9-10 is God's recommended standard for dress for women: "Adorn themselves in modest apparel, with propriety and moderation, not with braided hair or gold or pearls or costly clothing, but, which is proper for women professing godliness, with good works" (NKJV).

Modest dress can be defined in many ways as deemed by man, but when we search for God's definition, we find deeper meaning. The outer dress is the index of the inner mind. The Christian woman's dress should befit her Christian profession. She should reflect modesty in mind and saintliness in dress. We are soldiers, and as such, we are to dress accordingly. Loose-fitting clothing is much more appropriate than clothes that cling. Therefore, always dress for battle, and let what you wear always be decent and in order.

In my opinion, the best translation of 1 Timothy 2:9, as relates to the deaconess, is found in George M. Lamsa's translation of the Holy Bible from the Aramaic of the Peshitta, which reads, "In like manner also, let the apparel of women be simple and their adornment be modest and refined; not with braided hair or gold or pearls or costly array[11]." What attracts me to this translation is the use of the word "refined." Refined implies a certain level of self-respect that can only be brought about by maturity. Perhaps the only attribute that differentiates a Bible scholar from a deaconess is maturity. The apostle Paul wrote in 1 Corinthians 13:11, "When I was a child, I spake as a child, I thought as a child: but when I became a man, I put away childish things." Thus, a deaconess must rise above the sometimes youthful, carnal intrigue that comes from exciting the carnal nature of men with one's body. If we are to lead the church to higher moral grounds, we as virtuous women must to put away childish flirtations—the self-flattering, teasing of men—that are wrought by seductive apparel.

The braided hair, gold, pearls, and costly attire reference is further emphasis that we must adorn ourselves in a way that is "proper for women professing godliness, with good works." Good works are the best ornament, and they hold great value in the sight of God. Therefore, we must wear clothing that suggests virtue. This means loose clothing according to your size and style. Skin care is also important. Never hide your beauty by wearing heavy makeup—make up, not make over (moderation). Take good care of your skin, and for an even finish, use a foundation that enhances your beauty. Do not attempt to make yourself over. God has already created a beautiful product. Additionally, let us remember to adorn our heads as women professing godliness. Attention should be drawn to our inner beauty. In an era that is defined by brazen hair trends, the order of the day for deaconesses should be a style that reflects your profession. Our hats need not be seen before we are. Lastly, footwear should vary according to your size. Keep your feet in mind when you buy shoes. Take into consideration your profession and the style that is best suited for you. When in doubt, a pump will serve you well.

PREREQUISITES FOR DEACONESSES IN THE LOCAL CHURCH

Inner Beauty

1. What do you do daily to enhance your inner beauty?

   _____
   _____
   _____
   _____

2. How would you describe your personal fellowship with God?

   _____
   _____
   _____

3. How would you describe your stewardship as relates to . . .

   a) Time

   _____
   _____

b) Tithe

_____

_____

c) Talents

_____

_____

4. What is God saying to you in regards to self-denial?

_____

_____

_____

5. Is Christ a priority in your life? If so, how do you demonstrate this fact?

_____

_____

_____

6. Related to your conversation, would anyone label you a . . . (Check all that apply to you)

[ ] Gossiper
[ ] Slanderer
[ ] Having a sharp tongue
[ ] Loud
[ ] Silly
[ ] Exhorter
[ ] Trifler
[ ] Edifier

7. Have you ever been described as *wise*? If so, what was the specific occasion?

   _____

   _____

   _____

8. List three of your favorite passages of Scripture.

   a) _____
   b) _____
   c) _____

9. Are you a woman of faith? Explain.

   _____

   _____

   _____

10. Describe your prayer life.

    _____

    _____

    _____

Companions in Wisdom

1. What do the following passages from Proverbs teach about wisdom?

   a. 14:1 _____

   b. 14:3 _____

c. 14:24 _____
d. 14:35 _____
e. 15:2 _____
f. 15:7 _____
g. 15:12 _____
h. 15:24 _____
i. 15:31 _____
j. 16:21 _____
k. 17:28 _____
l. 18:15 _____
m. 19:20 _____
n. 20:1 _____
o. 21.11 _____
p. 21:20 _____
q. 22:17 _____
r. 24:6 _____
s. 25:12 _____
t. 26:5 _____
u. 26:12 _____
v. 28:11 _____

2. What are the four things that are little upon the earth, but are exceedingly wise? Why?

   a. _____
   b. _____
   c. _____

d. _____

3. As a deaconess, explain how important prayer is in your life?

   _____
   _____
   _____
   _____
   _____
   _____

4. Do you set aside any specific time of the day for prayer? If so, when?

   _____
   _____
   _____
   _____
   _____

5. Give an instance in which you have witnessed the power of prayer.

   _____
   _____
   _____
   _____
   _____
   _____

Prayer and the Deaconess

Deaconesses must be prayerful (use KJV for prompts)

1. Jesus' admonition to pray (Luke 18:1)

    "men ought _____ to _____, and not to _____."

2. The assurance of prayer (Matthew 21:22)

    "And _____ things, whatsoever ye shall ask in _____, _____, ye shall _____."

3. The need of prayer among the people of God (II Chronicles 7:14)

    If _____ people, which are called by my name, shall _____ themselves, and _____, and _____ my face, and _____ from their ways; then will I _____ from heaven, and will _____ their _____, and will _____ their land."

4. The power of prayer among the sick. (James 5:14-15a)

    Is any sick among you? let him call for the elders of the church; and let them pray over him, anointing him with oil in the name of the Lord: And the _____ of _____ shall _____ the _____, and the Lord shall _____ him up."

5. The prayer life of the Savior (Mark 1:35)

    "And in the _____, rising up a great while before

_____ , he went out, and departed into a _____ place, and there _____."

(Luke 6:12)
"And it came to pass in those days, that he went out into a mountain to _____, and continued all _____ in _____ to God."

6. Our readiness to pray (Romans 12:12)
   "Rejoicing in hope; patient in tribulation; continuing _____ in _____."

7. Encouragement to pray (Philippians 4:6)
   "Be careful for nothing; but in _____ by _____ and _____ with _____ let your _____ be made known unto God."

Hindrances to prayer

When prayers are not answered, you should examine yourself in the light of God's Word. If you find anything not pleasing to God, confess it—believing God for forgiveness—that your prayers may be answered (1 John 1:9). Keep in mind:

- An unharmonious relationship between husband and wife will hinder prayer (I Peter 3:1-7)
- Selfishness will hinder prayer (James 4:3)
- An unforgiving spirit will hinder prayer. Many Christians

go without answers to prayer because they have wronged others, or have been wronged, and have failed to humble themselves and seek reconciliation (Matthew 5:22-24)

- Unbelief will hinder prayer (James 1:6-7; Hebrews 11:6)

- Known sin in the heart will hinder prayer (Isaiah 59:1, 2; Psalm 66:18)

When you pray, go to God in all humility. Ask Him to reveal anything in your life that is not pleasing to Him. Then, judge it; confess it, calling it by name; and forsake it. Pray in all simplicity and earnestness—believing—and God will hear and answer.

18 Reasons for Unanswered Prayer

1. Refusing to hear truth (Proverbs 28:9)
2. Refusing to humble self (II Chronicles 7:14)
3. Forsaking God (II Chronicles 15:2)
4. Provoking God (Deuteronomy 3:26)
5. Hardheartedness (Zechariah 7:12-13)
6. Lack of charity (Proverbs 21:13)
7. Iniquity in the heart (Psalms 66:18)
8. Wrong motives (James 4:3)
9. Dishonor of companion (I Peter 3:7)
10. Unbelief (Matthew 17:20-21, 21:22)
11. Sin (James 4:1-5; John 9:31; Isaiah 59:2)
12. Parading prayer life (Matthew 6:5)
13. Vain repetitions (Matthew 6:7)
14. Unforgiveness (Matthew 6:14-15; Mark 11:25-26)
15. Hypocrisy (Luke 18:1-8)
16. Being discouraged (Luke 18:1-8)

17. Worry and anxiety (Philippians 4:6)
18. Doubting/double-mindedness (James 1:5-8)

Being Spirit-Filled

1. After reading the section on the deaconess being spirit-filled, what are your own thoughts?

   _____
   _____
   _____

2. How does it feel to be spirit-filled?

   _____
   _____
   _____

3. Write your personal experience regarding your own spirit-filling.

   _____
   _____
   _____

4. What is the difference in being *baptized in the Spirit* and in being *filled with the Spirit*?

   _____
   _____
   _____

Selecting Deaconesses

1. What requirement(s) would you add?
   _____
   _____
   _____

2. Do you think the dress code in 1 Timothy 2:9 is too restrictive? [ ] Yes or [ ] No
   Explain.
   _____
   _____
   _____

3. Not restrictive enough? [ ] Yes or [ ] No
   Explain.
   _____
   _____
   _____

4. Would the list of prerequisites in this chapter fit the congregation of which you are a member? [ ] Yes or [ ] No
   Explain.
   _____
   _____
   _____

Section V

THE SERVICE OF DEACONESSES

Let everything you do reflect the integrity and seriousness of your teaching. Teach the truth so that your teaching can't be criticized. Then those who oppose us will be ashamed and have nothing bad to say about us.

Titus 2:7b-8, NLT

ADMINISTRATION OF ORDINANCES

Baptism

In most churches, deaconesses assist in preparing candidates for baptism. The administrative duty of the deaconess begins immediately after a female candidate responds to the invitation to Christian discipleship. An informed deaconess is the best individual in the church to interview a female who has responded to the invitation. It is my personal conviction that it takes a woman to minister to a woman. A woman knows the pain of women. A woman knows the needs of women. A woman can hug and hold and wipe the tears of a woman in a manner that ministers to her. A church that allows men to receive and interview female candidates runs the risk of impropriety. When women respond to Christ, they are often emotional and possibly in their most vulnerable state. Deaconesses are best qualified to respond to their needs at that time, whereas men, regardless of how spiritual, are susceptible to sensual allurement.

The discipleship interview should be one of listening on the part of the interviewing deaconess. The candidate should be allowed to express her response to the invitation, as opposed to being barraged with pressurized evangelism. The overzealous deaconess can turn off a prospective disciple.

After the candidate expresses herself, it is the deaconess' responsibility to gently lead her down the road to discipleship. This should be a compassionate process with emphasis on the agape love of Christ. The interview ought to conclude with prayer and a follow-up date tentatively set, preferably within three days. It has been my experience that contact within 72 hours eliminates the possibility of the candidate being lost.

Baptism is the believer's act of obedience. Baptism does not save, but it is testimony to the fact one has received Jesus Christ as her Savior. Instruction should be given to the candidate.

Preparation:
- Inform candidate of baptism date
- Advise on proper attire
- Accompany the candidate to a warm, well-prepared room
- Ensure privacy
- At the proper time, accompany the candidate to the sanctuary
- Present candidate to the pastor for baptism according to the procedures of that particular church
- Immediately wrap the candidate, for health and reasons of propriety
- Accompany candidate back to dressing area and ensure privacy

"After Care" with the New Convert

Follow-up is extremely important for new babes in Christ. Follow-up is an area that needs much attention in most churches. As newborn infants need milk and continual nurturing to grow, new babes in Christ need to be fed a steady diet of the Word of God by a caring, seasoned disciple. Women naturally nurture. Therefore, who best to nurture female candidates than female disciples?

The Lord's Supper

As companion workers, the deaconesses in the Missionary Baptist Church are helpers and coworkers of the deacon's ministry. As such, deaconesses are responsible for the preparation of the table of the Lord's Supper. Such preparation includes:

- Preparing and organizing the table on the day of the supper
- Ensuring that every item is clean and ready for use:
  - White linen table cloth
  - Glasses
  - Trays
  - White gloves for the ministers and the deacons

To ensure an atmosphere of reverence, the table preparations begin with prayer. Idle or personal conversation is discouraged. The Lord's Supper is a sacred ordinance, and even its preparation should be done with reverence. Remember that the bread and wine represent the sacred body and precious blood of our Lord.

Disengage in outside activity during the preparation. When we ask Jesus to come see about us, would we want Him to be preoccupied with His own need? The business of tending to the table should remind our hearts and minds of the reason for this preparation.

"Let all things be done decently and in order."
I Corinthians 14:40

Benevolence

Occasion often arises when someone in the congregation needs assistance in the area of food, clothing, or shelter. Deaconesses may be called upon to assist deacons in determining what need, if any, should be provided. When that need is requested by a female member of the congregation, it is essential that a deaconess accompany the deacon in the investigation and evaluation process. No deaconess should allow a male officer (pastor, deacon, or trustee) to visit a female member of the congregation alone. The very presence of the deaconess will help to avoid the appearance of impropriety. The presence of a deaconess can also prevent the manipulation of a naïve male officer of the church by a female member who is bent on defrauding the church of resources set aside for the needy.

In many cases, deaconesses are also needed to provide home care for elderly or sick congregation members. Many health care plans do not provide around-the-clock home care. Most plans only provide four to six hours of home nursing care. A deaconess can be the vital link in such care. A deaconess can be called upon to provide essential housekeeping services and bedside assistance for the sick and shut-in. This care should also consist of house cleaning, food preparation, Bible reading, and prayer.

Counseling of Youth

Though it may be sad to say, there are children in every congregation who are not privileged or blessed with the relationship of a godly mother. God, in His wise providence, provides such a relationship in the form of a committed deaconess. Youth from the nursery to the college dorm can benefit from the motherly ministry of the deaconesses. Such relationships can be equally beneficial and rewarding to both youth and deaconess alike. It is often a hand on the shoulder, a hug, or simply a word of encouragement that gives some troubled youth reason to follow Christ. The deaconess must be alert for every opportunity to minister to the youth of the church. Good deaconesses nurture every member of the congregation.

Counseling of Men

A deaconess can provide male members of the congregation with feminine insight on problems pertaining to women. Many marriages have failed simply because husbands were not sensitive to the needs and feelings of their wives. Many teenage dating relationships have resulted in disaster or date rape because young men have not been taught how to relate to young women. Many male pastors are not meeting the needs of the female population of the church because they are not sensitive to the feelings, emotions, or issues pertaining to women. Every male member of the congregation ought to be blessed with the godly feminine advice and insight a deaconess can provide.

In reading Titus 2:6-8, I am not entirely convinced that Paul was not advising the older women to "exhort [encourage] the young men to be sober-minded, in all things showing [themselves] to be a pattern of good works; in doctrine showing integrity, reverence, incorruptibility, sound speech that cannot be condemned" (NKJV).

THIS DO IN REMEMBERANCE OF ME

I have found there are several principles that a deaconess must keep in mind as she goes throughout her ministry. I have included here the principles as well as scriptural support for these principles.

1. *The cause of Jesus Christ comes first*
   Matthew 10:37; Luke 14:26-27; Revelation 1:8

2. *God has the power, if you have the faith*
   Mark 9:23; Mark 11:22-24

3. *Pray and forgive*
   Mark 11:24-26

4. *Pray one for another*
   James 5:16

5. *Remember Lot's wife*
   Luke 17:32-33

6. *Be a good listener*
   Isaiah 50:5; St. Matthew 11:15

7. *Work with diligence*
   Proverbs 6:6; Proverbs 18:9

8. *Be timely*
   Ecclesiastes 3:1-8; Ephesians 5:16

9. *Be a friend*
   Proverbs 18:24

10. *A friend loveth at all times*
    Proverbs 17:17

11. *God does wonders with little things*
    St. Luke 12:32; 1 Kings 18:44

12. *Your gift will make room for you*
    Proverbs 18:16

13. *Pride will bring you low, but humility will lift you up*
    Proverbs 18:12

14. *Be happy*
    Philippians 4:4

STANDARDS FOR DEACONESSES

In the fall of 1996, my pastor issued a *New Standard for Deaconesses*. This new standard was designed to change the criteria by which deaconesses would be added to the ministry. This new standard was initially met with reservation and coolness, for it signaled that never again will deaconesses be selected and added to the ministry to *sit*, but to *serve*.

This new standard came as a surprise to many, but I could see its necessity long before it was officially documented in 1996. Since the early 1970s, I have seen the need for working, ministering, active deaconesses getting greater and greater as wounded women of all ages gravitated toward the church.

It was in the 1970s that the loose living, free loving, it's-your-thing-do-what-you-wanna-do policy of the 60s and 70s began to take its toll. Since the 1970s, we have begun to see the awful emotional, psychological, and spiritual effects of living life without God's guidance. The chickens certainly have come home to roost. The bill for the silence of the church of the 60s and 70s has become due. This generation of deaconesses must not only have good hearts, but just as important, we must have good doctrine.

My pastor's new standard takes into consideration that the educational level of deaconesses varies, but if we are to meet the challenge that this generation of hurting, wounded women presents, there must be new standards. The following is the edict of new standards presented by my pastor in September of 1996.

The New Standards for Deaconesses

As of this year, all deaconesses will be required to show evidence of a basic knowledge of Scripture and doctrine. Because of the new challenges as relates to the problems confronting women in our society today, and because there is a need for women to minister to women, deaconesses will have to be equipped with a basic knowledge of Scripture. In times gone by, the office of "deaconess" was considered an honor bestowed upon women who have shown a level of righteousness to simply recognize their past services. But today, the responsibilities of the deaconesses are essentially the same as the responsibilities of the deacons and ministers. Ministers are licensed after a trial or initial sermon and then are ordained at the proper time. Deacons are required to go through catechism and then stand before the congregation and ordination council to answer questions concerning their suitability for ordination.

If a deaconess is to be effective, at the very least, the congregation must have confidence in her ability to rightly divide the Word of Truth.

Heretofore, the candidates for deaconesses were required to do very little to demonstrate their suitability for the office insofar as a basic knowledge of God's Word. This has resulted in a lack of confidence on the part of the congregation as relates to deaconesses. If a deaconess is to be effective, at the very least, the congregation must have confidence in her ability to rightly divide the Word of Truth.

Thus, as of this year, deaconesses will be required to give public evidence of their knowledge of Scripture. The exact forum has not yet been decided. (See Appendix for sample.)

THE SERVICE OF DEACONESSES

1. What are the three primary areas of responsibility of a deaconess?

   a. _____

   b. _____

   c. _____

2. As relates to baptism, the deaconess' responsibility is primarily to the _____ candidates.

3. List the 8 points of concern as relates to the day of baptism.

   a. _____

   b. _____

   c. _____

   d. _____

   e. _____

   f. _____

   g. _____

   h. _____

4. What follow-up care should be given to new converts by the deaconess?

   _____
   _____
   _____

5. Describe the duties of the deaconess as relates to preparation of the Lord's Supper.

   _____
   _____
   _____

6. In the area of benevolence, why is it advisable for a deaconess to accompany her pastor or a deacon to investigate and evaluate insofar as women are concerned?

   _____
   _____
   _____

7. What should be the source of the counsel you give?

   _____
   _____
   _____

8. Read and explain Matthew 20:27.

   _____
   _____

9. In what ways do you attempt to practice servitude?
   _____
   _____

10. Specifically, how do you demonstrate a servant's spirit as relates to your . . .

    a. Pastor
       _____
       _____

    b. Deacons
       _____
       _____

    c. President of Deaconesses
       _____
       _____

    d. Fellow Deaconesses
       _____
       _____

    e. Church Mothers
       _____
       _____

    f. Fellow Church Members
       _____
       _____

Afterword

Every now and then, in the secret chambers of my heart, I ponder the horrible *what if* questions. What if deaconesses don't respond to this call to arms? What if deaconesses revert to the ceremonial do-nothing ways of the past few decades? What if deaconesses choose to continue to major in ceremony and minor in ministry? What if the lukewarm conditions of this church era continue throughout the 21st century?

If deaconesses in this generation do not respond to the clarion call of the Holy Spirit to reach out to young women, the results will be devastating. In the house of God, I see an upsurge of lesbianism, drug addiction, and depression, and a menagerie of psychological problems associated with pain of being ministerially neglected. I see ministers falling from grace as they become entangled in the web of doing what God intended for women. I see the church of the 21st century overrun with wounded women and weary men trying to cope with their ignorance. I see a painful continuation of the improprieties that have plagued evangelical ministries as well as the Catholic church over the past several years.

The very thought of these questions is too horrible to imagine because if the church chooses to continue with a "business as usual" policy, then unborn generations will be the victims of the slothfulness of this generation. As I peer into the future through the spiritual telescope of God's prophets, I see a horrendous decline of our daughters to an unparalleled dimension of immorality.

Finally, I see the church, as we know it today, slipping into oblivion as it becomes irrelevant to future generations because it refuses to tackle the difficult problems of this age. So, my sister deaconesses, we have our backs against the wall. Will we come out swinging the sword of the Spirit, or will we crumble under the weight of Satan's final assault? I am not desiring to be a prophet of doom, but I believe it's a *now or never, do or die, put up or shut up* situation we're dealing with. Which ones of us will stand up against the popular tide of immorality of this generation and dare to reach out to drowning women with a hand of love and a word from the Lord? Will we, as deaconesses, respond to the ageless query from the heavens, "Who shall we send?" "Who shall go for us?" Or, will these questions of divine consequence be met with the deafening silence of fear and apathy? I shudder to imagine what will happen if enough of us do not respond, "Lord, here am I, send me."

Appendices

Helpful Scriptural References for Counseling

1. When visiting the sick

    Psalm 39:12-13:
    Hear my prayer, O Lord, and give ear unto my cry; hold not thy peace at my tears; for I am a stranger with thee, and a sojourner, as all my fathers were. spare me, that I may recover strength, before I go hence, and be no more.

    Psalm 103:1-5:
    Bless the Lord, O my soul: and all that is within me, bless his holy name. Bless the Lord, O my soul, and forget not all his benefits: Who forgiveth all thine iniquities; who healeth all thy diseases; Who redeemeth thy life from destruction; who crowneth thee with loving kindness and tender mercies; Who satisfieth thy mouth with good things; so that thy youth is renewed like the eagle's.

    (See also Psalms 25:16-18; Psalms 43:2-5; Psalms 46:1-2, 10 (emphasize 1 & 2); Psalms 23; Isaiah 45:22)

2. When falsely accused

    Psalm 27:12-14:
    Deliver me not over unto the will of mine enemies: for false witnesses are risen up against me, and such as breathe out cruelty. I had fainted, unless I had believed to see the goodness of the Lord in the land of the living. Wait on the Lord: be of good courage, and

he shall strengthen thine heart: wait, I say, on the Lord.

Matthew 5:8-9:
Blessed are the pure in heart: for they shall see God. Blessed are the peacemakers: for they shall be called the. children of God.

3. When in need of guidance

Psalm 25:1-5:
Unto thee, O Lord, do I lift up my soul. O my God, I trust in thee: let me not be ashamed, let not mine enemies triumph over me. Yea, let none that wait on thee be ashamed: let them be ashamed which transgress without cause. Shew me thy ways, a Lord; teach me thy paths. Lead me in thy truth, and teach me: for thou art the God of my salvation; on thee do I wait all the day.

Psalm 27:10-11:
When my father and my mother forsake me, then the Lord will take me up. Teach me thy way, a Lord, and lead me in a plain path, because of mine enemies.

(See also Psalm 121)

4. When recovering from illness

Psalm 30:1-12:
I will extol thee, a Lord; for thou has lifted me up, and hast not made my foes to rejoice over me. O Lord my God, I cried unto thee, and thou hast healed me. O Lord, thou hast brought up my soul from the grave: thou hast kept me alive, that I should not go down to the pit. Sing unto the Lord, O ye saints of his, and give thanks at the remembrance of his holiness. For his anger endureth but a moment; in his favour is life: weeping may endure for a night, but joy cometh in the morning. And in my prosperity I said, I shall never be moved. Lord, by thy favour thou hast made my mountain to stand strong: thou didst hide thy face, and I was troubled. I cried

to thee, a Lord; and unto the Lord I made supplication. What profit is there in my blood, when I go down to the pit? Shall the dust praise thee? Shall it declare thy truth? Hear, O Lord, and have mercy upon me: Lord, be thou my helper. Thou hast turned for me my mourning into dancing: thou hast put off my sackcloth, and girded me with gladness; To the end that my glory may sing praise to thee, and not be silent. a Lord my God, I will give thanks unto thee for ever.*

(See also Psalm 40:1-5; Psalm 91:1-7)

5. When in need of forgiveness

    Psalm 25:6-7:
    Remember, O Lord, thy tender mercies and thy loving kindnesses; for they have been ever of old. Remember not the sins of my youth, nor my transgressions: according to thy mercy remember thou me for thy goodness' sake, O Lord.

    Psalm 39:7-11:
    And now, Lord, what wait I for? my hope is in thee. Deliver me from all my transgressions: make me not the reproach of the foolish. I was dumb, I opened not my mouth; because thou didst it. Remove thy stroke away from me: I am consumed by the blow of thine hand. When thou with rebukes dost correct man for iniquity, thou makest his beauty to consume away like a moth: surely every man is vanity. Selah.

6. The blessedness of forgiveness

    Psalm 32:1-5:
    Blessed is he whose transgression is forgiven, whose sin is covered. Blessed is the man unto whom the Lord imputeth not iniquity, and in whose spirit there is no guile. When I kept silence, my bones waxed old through my roaring all the day long. For day and night thy hand was heavy upon me: my moisture is turned into the

drought of summer. Selah. I acknowledged my sin unto thee, and mine iniquity have I not hid. I said, I will confess my transgressions unto the Lord; and thou forgavest the iniquity of my sin. Selah.

Isaiah 43:25:
I, even L am he that blotteth out thy transgressions for mine own sake, and will not remember thy sins.

Isaiah 44:22:
I have blotted out, as a thick cloud, thy transgressions, and, as a cloud, thy sins: return unto me; for I have redeemed thee.

7. When delivered from trouble

Psalm 34:1-9:
I will bless the Lord at all times: his praise shall continually be in my mouth. My soul shall make her boast in the Lord: the humble shall hear thereof, and be glad. O magnify the Lord with me, and let us exalt his name together. I sought the Lord, and he heard me, and delivered me from all my fears. They looked unto him, and were lightened: and their faces were not ashamed. This poor man cried, and the Lord heard him, and saved him out of all his troubles. The angel of the Lord encampeth round about them that fear him, and delivereth them. O taste and see that the Lord is good: blessed is the man that trusteth in him. fear the Lord, ye his saints: for there is no want to them that fear him.

(See also Psalm 92:1-5; Psalm 150)

8. When the wicked have much, and you have little

Psalm 37:16-24:
A little that a righteous man hath is better than the riches of many wicked. For the arms of the wicked shall be broken: but the Lord upholdeth the righteous. The Lord knoweth the days of the upright: and their inheritance shall be for ever. They shall not be ashamed in the evil time: and in the days of famine they shall be

satisfied. But the wicked shall perish, and the enemies of the Lord shall be as the fat of lambs: they shall consume; into smoke shall they consume away. The wicked borroweth, and payeth not again: but the righteous sheweth mercy, and giveth. For such as be blessed of him shall inherit the earth; and they that be cursed of him shall be cut off. The steps of a good man are ordered by the Lord: and he delighteth in his way. Though he fall, he shall not be utterly cast down: for the Lord upholdeth him with his hand.

(See also Psalm 49:12-20)

9. When enemies plot against the faithful

    Psalm 35:1-3:
    Plead my cause, O Lord, with them that strive with me: fight against them that fight against me. Take hold of shield and buckler, and stand up for mine help. Draw out also the spear, and stop the way against them that persecute me: say unto my soul, I am thy salvation.

    (See also verses 4-23)

    Psalm 38:19-22:
    But mine enemies are lively, and they are strong: and they that hate me wrongfully are multiplied. They also that render evil for good are mine adversaries; because I follow the thing that good is. Forsake me not, O Lord: O my God, be not far from me.
    Make haste to help me, O Lord my salvation.

    (See also Isaiah 41:10-12)

10. When given to anger

    Psalm 37:7-15:
    Rest in the Lord, and wait patiently for him: fret not thyself because of him who prospereth in his way, because of the man who bringeth wicked devices to pass. Cease from anger, and forsake

wrath: fret not thyself in any wise to do evil. For evildoers shall be cut off: but those that wait upon the Lord, they shall inherit the earth. For yet a little while, and the wicked shall not be: yea, thou shalt diligently consider his place, and it shall not be. But the meek shall inherit the earth; and shall delight themselves in the abundance of peace. The wicked plotteth against the just, and gnasheth upon him with his teeth. The Lord shall laugh at him: for he seeth that his day is coming. The wicked have drawn out the sword, and have bent their bow, to cast down the poor and needy, and to slay such as be of upright conversation. Their sword shall enter into their own heart, and their bows shall be broken. A little that a righteous man hath is better than the riches of many wicked. For the arms of the wicked shall be broken: but the Lord upholdeth the righteous.

(See also Deuteronomy 32:35; Psalm 94:1; Proverbs 6:34; Proverbs 16:32; Ecclesiastes 7:9; Isaiah 63:4; Romans 12:19; Hebrews 10:30)

11. When in danger or trouble

    Psalm 31:1-2:
    In thee, O Lord, do I put my trust; let me never be ashamed: deliver me in thy righteousness. Bow down thine ear to me; deliver me speedily: be thou my strong rock, for an house of defence to save me.

    Isaiah 49:1-2:
    Listen, O isles, unto me; and hearken, ye people, from far; The Lord hath called me from the womb; from the bowels of my mother hath he made mention of my name. And he hath made my mouth like a sharp sword; in the shadow of his hand hath he hid me, and made me a polished shaft; in his quiver hath he hid me.

    (See also Psalm 23; Psalm 27; Isaiah 45:2; Isaiah 54:17)

12. Trust and faith in God

    Psalm 23:1:
    The Lord is my shepherd; I shall not want.

    Proverbs 3:5-6:
    Trust in the Lord with all thine heart; and lean not unto thine own understanding. In all thy ways acknowledge him, and he shall direct thy paths.

    Lamentations 3:22:
    It is of the Lord's mercies that we are not consumed, because his compassions fail not.

    Psalm 46:1:
    God is our refuge and strength, a very present help in trouble.

    Nahum 1:7:
    The Lord is good, a strong hold in the day of trouble; and he knoweth them that trust in him.

13. When encouraging righteousness

    Psalm 37:37-40:
    Mark the perfect man, and behold the upright: for the end of that man is peace. But the transgressors shall be destroyed together: the end of the wicked shall be cut off. But the salvation of the righteous is of the Lord: he is their strength in the time of trouble. And the Lord shall help them, and deliver them: he shall deliver them from the wicked, and save them, because they trust in him.

    Isaiah 51:7-8:
    Hearken unto me, ye that know righteousness, the people in whose heart is my law; fear ye not the reproach of men, neither be ye afraid of their revilings. For the moth shall eat them up like a garment, and the worm shall eat them like wool: but my righteous-

ness shall be for ever; and my salvation from generation to generation.

Isaiah 51:1-3:
Hearken to me, ye that follow after righteousness, ye that seek the Lord: look unto the rock whence ye are hewn, and to the hole of the pit whence ye are digged. Look unto Abraham your father; and unto Sarah that bare you: for I called him alone, and blessed him, and increased him. For the Lord shall comfort Zion: he will comfort all her waste places; and he will make her wilderness like Eden, and her desert like the garden of the Lord; joy and gladness shall be found therein, thanksgiving, and the voice of melody.

(See also Isaiah 51:10-12; Isaiah 56:2; Isaiah 33:1-5)

14. When a faithful person is in need of God's help

Psalm 40:8-17:
I delight to do thy will, O my God: yea, thy law is within my heart. I have preached righteousness in the great congregation: lo, I have not refrained my lips, O Lord, thou knowest. I have not hid thy righteousness within my heart; I have declared thy faithfulness and thy salvation: I have not concealed thy lovingkindness and thy truth from the great congregation. Withhold not thou thy tender mercies from me, O Lord: let thy lovingkindness and thy truth continually preserve me. For innumerable evils have compassed me about: mine iniquities have taken hold upon me, so that I am not able to look up; they are more than the hairs of mine head: therefore my heart faileth me. Be pleased, O Lord, to deliver me: O Lord, make haste to help me. Let them be ashamed and confounded together that seek after my soul to destroy it; let them be driven backward and put to shame that wish me evil. Let them be desolate for a reward of their shame that say unto me, Aha, aha. Let all those that seek thee rejoice and be glad in thee: let such as love thy salvation say continually, The Lord be magnified. But I am poor and needy; yet the Lord thinketh upon me: thou art my help and my deliverer; make no tarrying, O my God.

Isaiah 54:14-17:

In righteousness shalt thou be established: thou shalt be far from oppression; for thou shalt not fear: and from terror; for it shall not come near thee. Behold, they shall surely gather together, but not by me: whosoever shall gather together against thee shall fall for thy sake. Behold, I have created the smith that bloweth the coals in the fire, and that bringeth forth an instrument for his work; and I have created the waster to destroy. No weapon that is formed against thee shall prosper; and every tongue that shall rise against thee in judgment thou shalt condemn. This is the heritage of the servants of the Lord, and their righteousness is of me, saith the Lord.

15. When the tongue needs control

Psalm 39:1:

I said, I will take heed to my ways, that I sin not with my tongue: I will keep my mouth with a bridle, while the wicked is before me.

James 3:2-10:

For in many things we offend all. If any man offend not in word, the same is a perfect man, and able also to bridle the whole body. Behold, we put bits in the horses' mouths, that they may obey us; and we turn about their whole body. Behold also the ships, which though they be so great, and are driven of fierce winds, yet are they turned about with a very small helm, whithersoever the governor listeth. Even so the tongue is a little member, and boasteth great things. Behold, how great a matter a little fire kindleth! And the tongue is a fire, a world of iniquity: so is the tongue among our members, that it defileth the whole body, and setteth on fire the course of nature; and it is set on fire of hell. For every kind of beasts, and of birds, and of serpents, and of things in the sea, is tamed, and hath been tamed of mankind: But the tongue can no man tame; it is an unruly evil, full of deadly poison. Therewith bless we God, even the Father; and therewith curse we men, which are made after the similitude of God. Out of the same mouth proceedeth blessing and cursing. My brethren, these things ought not so to be.

Proverbs 18:6-8:
A fool's lips enter into contention, and his mouth calleth for strokes. A fool's mouth is his destruction, and his lips are the snare of his soul. The words of a talebearer are as wounds, and they go down into the innermost parts of the belly.

(Liars love to listen to lies: See also Proverbs 17:4)

16. When the charitable need help

Psalm 41:7-13:
All that hate me whisper together against me: against me do they devise my hurt. An evil disease, say they, cleaveth fast unto him: and now that he lieth he shall rise up no more. Yea, mine own familiar friend, in whom I trusted, which did eat of my bread, hath lifted up his heel against me. But thou, O Lord, be merciful unto me, and raise me up, that I may requite them. By this I know that thou favourest me, because mine enemy doth not triumph over me. And as for me, thou upholdest me in mine integrity, and settest me before thy face for ever: Blessed be the Lord God of Israel from everlasting, and to everlasting. Amen, and Amen.

17. When encouraging prayer

Psalm 55:17:
Evening, and morning, and at noon, will I pray, and cry aloud: and he shall hear my voice.

Psalm 64:1:
Hear my voice, O God, in my prayer: preserve my life from fear of the enemy.

Matthew 26:41:

Watch and pray, that ye enter not into temptation: the spirit indeed is willing, but the flesh is weak.

1 Peter 3:12:

For the eyes of the Lord are over the righteous, and his ears are open unto their prayers: but the face of the Lord is against them that do evil.

(See also Psalm 61:1-4; Psalm 62:5-8; Psalm 65:2; Isaiah 45:22; Luke 18:1; St. Luke 11:1; Isaiah 56:7; James 5:3; 1 Thessalonians 5:17; 1 Thessalonians 3:10)

18. When in need of strength

Isaiah 46:4:

And even to your old age I am he; and even to hoar hairs will I carry you: I have made, and I will bear; even I will carry, and will deliver you.

Isaiah 40:10:

Behold, the Lord God will come with strong hand, and his arm shall rule for him: behold, his reward is with him, and his work before him.

Isaiah 41:10:

Fear thou not; for I am with thee: be not dismayed; for I am thy God: I will strengthen thee; yea, I will help thee; yea, I will uphold thee with the right hand of my righteousness.

(See also Psalm 105:1-5; Psalm 127; Psalm 150; Psalm 116:1-7; Psalm 119:57-64)

Consecration Examination

(SAMPLE)

OPENING INQUIRY

Share Your Salvation Experience
(Candidate is to share with the congregation her conversion experience, giving dates, circumstances, and all pertinent information.)

1. As relates to your husband's ministry as deacon, what is your responsibility as his wife?

   Answer: My responsibility as my husband's wife in his ministry as a deacon is the same responsibility I have for him as his wife for life, and that is to be a "help meet," and not a hindrance to him.

   Genesis 2:18, "And the Lord God said, It is not good that the man should be alone; I will make a help meet for him."

2. Who is the head in your home?

   Answer: My husband is the head in our home.

   Ephesians 5:22-24 states:

   Wives, submit yourselves unto your own husbands, as unto

the Lord. For the husband is the head of the wife, even as Christ is the head of the church: and he is the saviour of the body. Therefore as the church is subject unto Christ, so let the wives be to their own husbands in every thing.

3. Does that mean he should be a dictator in the home?

    <u>Answer</u>: No, it simply means that I am to give him the respect and fidelity he is due as my husband, and to follow him as he follows Christ.

4. Does Scripture say anything in regards to the conduct of a deacon's wife?

    <u>Answer</u>: Yes, the Bible is very specific as relates to the conduct of a deacon's wife.

    1 Timothy 3:11 states:

    Even so must their wives be grave, not slanderers, sober, faithful in all things.

5. What, if anything, does Scripture say in reference to rendering due benevolence to your husband?

    <u>Answer</u>: Scripture states that we ought to render due benevolence to each other.

    1 Corinthians 7:3-5 states:

    Let the husband render unto the wife due benevolence: and likewise also the wife unto the husband. The wife hath not power of her own body, but the husband: and likewise also the husband hath not power of his own body, but the wife. Defraud ye not one the other, except it be with consent for a time, that ye may give yourselves to fasting and prayer; and come together again, that Satan tempt you not for your incontinency.

6. What is your duty as relates to the younger women of the church?

   <u>Answer</u>: Scripture tells me that I am to teach the younger women in the church, first by example, then by precept.

   Titus 2:3 states:

   The aged women likewise, that they be in behaviour as becometh holiness, not false accusers, not given to much wine, teachers of good things.

7. What are you to teach them according to Titus 2:4-5?

   <u>Answer</u>: That they may teach the young women to be sober, to love their husbands, to love their children, To be discreet, chaste, keepers at home, good, obedient to their own husbands, that the word of God be not blasphemed.

8. Is it scriptural for a woman to teach a class that includes men?

   <u>Answer</u>: Yes, for teaching men does not confer authority over men. The teacher, as well as the preacher, are ministers. Ministers are servants. Thus, to teach or to preach is to serve, not to exercise authority.

9. Does the Scripture allow for women to pastor?

   Answer: There is a difference in the gift of pastoring and in the office of senior pastor. There is no evidence in Scripture for women "senior pastors," meaning shepherds over the entire flock of God, but the gift of pastoring has no respecter of persons. Every leader in the church ought to be endowed with the gift of pastoring.

10. What does 1 Timothy 2:12 mean when it states that "a woman ought not usurp authority over the man, but to be in silence."

    Answer: This was a specific message from Paul to a specific church with a specific problem of women usurping authority over men. It is generally accepted that the woman ought not debate or be argumentative in public, thereby becoming an embarrassment to Christ, the church, men of authority, or her husband. Let the differences between husband and wife be dealt with at home.

11. How ought a godly woman dress?

    Answer: According to I Timothy 2:9:

    Women ought to *adorn themselves in modest apparel, with shamefacedness and sobriety*.

12. What is the price of virtuous woman?

    Answer: According to Proverbs 31:10:

    Her price is far above rubies.

13. What is a "virtuous" woman?

    Answer: A woman displaying a Godly character, a love for her God, her husband, and her family.

14. According to 1 Corinthians, what can the sanctified wife do for the unbelieving husband?

    Answer: According to 1 Corinthians 7:14:

    The unbelieving husband is sanctified by the wife. The opposite is true as well: *The unbelieving wife is sanctified by the husband.*

15. Does God call women to preach?

    Answer: Joel 2:28-29 states:

    And it shall come to pass afterward, that I will pour out my spirit upon all flesh; and your sons and your daughters shall prophesy, your old men shall dream dreams, your young men shall see visions: And also upon the servants and upon the handmaids in those days will I pour out my spirit.

16. Who was Eve?

    Answer: 1) The first woman created, and 2) Adam's wife.

17. Who named Eve?

    Answer: Adam. Genesis 3:20 states:

    And Adam called his wife's name Eve; because she was the

mother of all living.

18. Who was Sarah?

    Answer: Sarah was Abraham's wife. She was also the mother of Isaac.

19. What was the mistake of Lot's wife?

    Answer: Looking back longingly to Sodom.

20. Who was Ruth?

    Answer: An ancestor of David and Jesus. The central character in the biblical book that bears her name.

21. What were the famous words that she uttered to her mother-in-law Naomi?

    Answer: Ruth 1:16:

    And Ruth said, Entreat me not to leave thee, or to return from following after thee: for whither thou goest, I will go; and where thou lodgest, I will lodge: thy people shall be my people, and thy God my God.

22. Who was Deborah?

    Answer: Deborah was prophetess and Judge of Israel during the period of Canaanite Oppression, about 1200 B.C. Her story can be found in the fifth chapter of Judges.

23. Who was Esther?

Answer: Esther was the central character in the Book of Esther. She was a Jewish, orphan girl who became queen of Persia. She saved her people from pure genocide.

24. What was Jesus' mother's name?

    Answer: Mary.

25. What was John the Baptist's mother's name?

    Answer: Elizabeth.

26. What were the names of Timothy's mother and grandmother?

    Answer: The mother and grandmother of Timothy are mentioned II Timothy 1:5:

    When I call to remembrance the unfeigned faith that is in thee, which dwelt first in thy grandmother Lois, and thy mother Eunice; and I am persuaded that in thee also.

27. Who was Phoebe?

    Answer: Phoebe was a co-laborer of Paul and is considered to be the first deaconess. Reference to her is found in the sixteenth chapter of Romans.

Biography

(SAMPLE)

Betsy Simmons, a native of Washington, MD, is the youngest of eight children born to the late Nadine Perry. She was educated through the Washington County Public School System.

Sister Simmons met Deacon Ernest Simmons in November 1970, and they were later married on June 22, 1973. She is the proud mother of four wonderful children: Kurt, Betina, Antoine, and Ernest II.

After being employed by the Federal Government from 1975 to 1990, she became a licensed child-care provider. Also in 1990, because of her love for children, she started her own daycare center in her home.

Betsy joined The True Word Baptist Church in 1990 and was baptized by Pastor Jon Martin. She is an active and-faithful member, having completed two Virtuous Women classes and currently acting as co-facilitator of class #6, Virtuous Women (Young Adults). She has served as an usher and treasurer for the Ushers' Ministry for several years. Sister Simmons has also served on the Hospitality Ministry as treasurer.

The passage of Scripture on which Sister Simmons stands is Psalm 32:8, "I will instruct thee and teach thee in the way which thou shalt go: I will guide thee with mine eye."

Deaconess Consecration Service

(SAMPLE)

ORDER OF SERVICE
Deaconess Ruth Brown, Presiding

Devotion	Deaconess/Mothers
Congregational	Hymn #329 "I Am Thine, O Lord"
Welcome & Occasion	Deaconess Carrie Hart
Selection	The Combined Choir
Presidential Statement	Deaconess Ann Jones
Presentation of Candidate Deaconess Faye Hall	
Candidate: Sister Betsy Simmons	
The Examination	Deaconess Ann Jones
Selection	Guest Choir
Offering	Deaconess
Charge to the Congregation	Minister Anne Cherry
Charge to the Deaconess	Deaconess Verna Ghee
Consecration Prayer	Minister Sharon Neal
Welcome into Deaconess Ministry	Deaconess Marie True
Introduction of Guest	Minister Deaconess Ann Jones
Selection	Guest Choir
The Gospel	Rev. Marion Biddle
	First Baptist Church
	Hope Well, Virginia
Invitation to Christian Discipleship	Minister Ida Day
Remarks	Deaconess Betsy Simmons
	Deacon Ernest Simmons
	Minister Sharon Neal
	Deaconess Ann Jones
	Deacon Frank Hurley
	Pastor Jon Martin

Presentation	Deaconess Jean Wooten
Closing Remarks	Rev. Marion Biddle
Benediction	Rev. Marion Biddle

Deaconesses Must be Servants

S   SAVED: "Let them alone: they be blind leaders of the blind. And if the blind lead the blind, both shall fall into the ditch." (Matthew 15:14)

E   ETHICAL: "Let all things be done decently and in order." (1 Corinthians 14:40)

     EXHORTERS: "But exhort one another daily, while it is called To day; lest any of you be hardened through the deceitfulness of sin." (Hebrews 3:13)

R   RELIABLE: But let your communication be, Yea, yea; Nay, nay: for whatsoever is more than these cometh of evil. (Matthew 5:37)

V   VIRTUOUS: "Who can find a virtuous woman? For her price is far above rubies." (Proverbs 31:10)

     "According as his divine power hath given unto us all things that pertain unto life and godliness, through the knowledge of him that hath called us to glory and virtue." (2 Peter 1:3)

     VISIONARIES: "Where there is no vision, the people perish: but he that keepeth the law, happy is he." (Proverbs 29:18)

A   ACCOUNTABLE: "Who shall give account to him that is ready to judge the quick and the dead." (1 Peter 4:5)

     Obey them that have the rule over you, and submit yourselves: for they watch for your souls, as they that must give account, that they may do it with joy, and not with grief: for that is unprofitable for you. (Hebrews 13:17)

N   NURTURERS: "And I, brethren, could not speak unto you as unto spiritual, but as unto carnal, even as unto babes in Christ. Jeremiah 3:15, And I will give you pastors according to mine heart, which shall feed you with knowledge and understanding." (1 Corinthians 3:1-2)

T   TEACHABLE: "That the aged men be sober, grave, temperate, sound in faith, in charity, in patience. The aged women likewise, that they be in behaviour as becometh holiness, not false accusers, not given to much wine, teachers of good things; That they may teach the young women to be sober, to love their husbands, to love their children, To be discreet, chaste, keepers at home, good, obedient to their own husbands, that the word of God be not blasphemed." (Titus 2:2-5)

S   SANCTIFIED: "Abstain from all appearance of evil. And the very God of peace sanctify you wholly; and I pray God your whole spirit and soul and body be preserved blameless unto the coming of our Lord Jesus Christ." (1 Thessalonians 5:22-23)

     STUDIOUS: "And the things that thou hast heard of me among many witnesses, the same commit thou to faithful men, who shall be able to teach others also." (2 Timothy 2:2)

Notes

1. H. Norman. Wright, *Healing for the Father Wound: A Trusted Christian Counselor Offers Time-Test Advice* (Minneapolis, MN: Bethany House, 2008).
2. Kathy Rodriquez, *Healing the Father Wound*, 2nd ed. (Createspace, 2004).
3. Margo Maine, *Father Hunger: Fathers, Daughters, and the Pursuit of Thinness* (Carlsbad, CA: Gurze Books, 2004).
4. Anand Prahlad, *African American Folklore: An Encyclopedia for Students* (Santa Barbara, CA: Greenwood, 2016).
5. Sally Kane, "Common Characteristics of Traditionalists (The Silent Generation)," The balance, March 20, 2017, accessed April 1, 2017, https://www.thebalance.com/workplace-characteristics-silent-generation-2164692.
6. I encourage deaconess to study the account of Beth Thomas in the documentary *Child of Rage*. *Child of Rage*, accessed May 10, 2017, https://documentarystorm.com/child-of-rage. Also study the attachment disorder work of her mother Nancy Thomas.
7. Joseph M. Scriven, "What A Friend We Have in Jesus," Hymnary, accessed April 12, 2017, http://hymnary.org/text/what_a_friend_we_have_in_jesus_all_our_s.
8. Spiritual, "There is a Balm in Gilead," Hymnary, accessed April 12, 2017, http://hymnary.org/text/sometimes_i_feel_discouraged_spiritual.
9. Jack W. Hayford, *God's Way to Wholeness: Divine Healing by the Power of the Holy Spirit* (Nashville, TN: T. Nelson, 1993), 49.
10. Alfred Lord Tennyson, "Morte d'Arthur," Poetry Foundation, accessed April 12, 2017, https://www.poetryfoundation.org/poems-and-poets/poems/detail/45370.
11. George Lamsa, "Peshitta New Testament," Dukhrana Biblical Research, accessed February 20, 2017, http://www.dukhrana.com/peshitta/index.php.

ABOUT THE AUTHOR

FRANCES "FRAN" A. JONES is a native of Charlotte, North Carolina. She is president of the Deaconess Ministry at The Word of God Baptist Church in Washington, DC, an instructor at Washington Baptist Seminary in Mount Rainier, Maryland, and founder and CEO of Imparting Grace Ministries (formerly FJ Dedicated Ministries, Inc.).

Fran earned a Master of Divinity degree from Washington Baptist Seminary and holds a Bachelor of Arts degree in Biblical Studies from Faith Christian Bible College and Schools in Washington, DC. She has also completed business administration coursework at Prince George's Community College and numerous courses and training in US government contracting techniques and Department of Defense installations. She is a retired employee of the federal government.

She is considered the nation's foremost authority on the work of deaconesses in the Baptist church, and she travels throughout the United States teaching and ministering to women of all ages through seminars and workshops. She is affectionately known as "a pastor's best friend," for her work in strengthening deaconesses is highly valued. She is the author of five books on the deaconess ministry: *The Making of a Deaconess*, *The Making of a Deaconess Workbook*, *Deaconesses Going Beyond the Communion Table*, *Called Out to Step Up to a Deaconess Ministry: A 12 –Step Program from Observation to Consecration*, and *The 21st Century Deaconess: Meeting the Urban Challenge*.

Fran is married to Earnest Jones, a native of Shreveport, Louisiana, and they have two children, Tina and Jerome, and eight grandchildren: Anaiah, Kamau, Dikembwe, Arikah, Anele Tharnell III, Aniyah, and Kyra.

www.ingramcontent.com/pod-product-compliance
Lightning Source LLC
Chambersburg PA
CBHW072030170426
43200CB00025B/2448